MISCARRIAG

Causes, consequences and remedies

Sam Poyser, Angus Nurse and Rebecca Milne

P

First published in Great Britain in 2018 by

Policy Press
University of Bristol
1-9 Old Park Hill
Bristol
BS2 8BB
UK
t: +44 (0)117 954 5940
pp-info@bristol.ac.uk
www.policypress.co.uk

North America office:
Policy Press
c/o The University of Chicago Press
1427 East 60th Street
Chicago, IL 60637, USA
t: +1 773 702 7700
f: +1 773-702-9756
sales@press.uchicago.edu
www.press.uchicago.edu

© Policy Press 2018

British Library Cataloguing in Publication Data
A catalogue record for this book is available from the British Library

Library of Congress Cataloging-in-Publication Data
A catalog record for this book has been requested

ISBN 978-1-4473-2744-8 paperback
ISBN 978-1-4473-2743-1 hardcover
ISBN 978-1-4473-2746-2 ePub
ISBN 978-1-4473-2747-9 Mobi
ISBN 978-1-4473-2745-5 ePdf

The right of Sam Poyser, Angus Nurse and Rebecca Milne to be identified as authors of this work has been asserted by them in accordance with the Copyright, Designs and Patents Act 1988.

All rights reserved: no part of this publication may be reproduced, stored in a retrieval system, or transmitted in any form or by any means, electronic, mechanical, photocopying, recording, or otherwise without the prior permission of Policy Press.

The statements and opinions contained within this publication are solely those of the authors and not of the University of Bristol or Policy Press. The University of Bristol and Policy Press disclaim responsibility for any injury to persons or property resulting from any material published in this publication.

Policy Press works to counter discrimination on grounds of gender, race, disability, age and sexuality.

Cover design by Policy Press
Front cover image: istock
Printed and bound in Great Britain by CPI Group (UK) Ltd,
Croydon, CR0 4YY
Policy Press uses environmentally responsible print partners

KEY THEMES IN POLICING

Series summary: This textbook series is designed to fill a growing need for titles which reflect the importance of incorporating 'evidence based policing' within Higher Education curriculums. It will reflect upon the changing landscape of contemporary policing as it becomes more politicised, professionalised and scrutinised, and draw out both change and continuities in its themes.

Series Editors: Dr Megan O'Neill, University of Dundee, Dr Marisa Silvestri, University of Kent and Dr Stephen Tong, Canterbury Christ Church University.

Published

Understanding police intelligence work – Adrian James

Plural policing – Colin Rogers

Key challenges in criminal investigation – Dr Martin O'Neill

Forthcoming

Practical psychology for policing – Dr Jason Roach

Towards ethical policing – Dominic Wood

Police accountability – Michael Rowe

Police culture – Tom Cockroft

Police leadership – Claire Davis and Marisa Silvestri

Editorial advisory board
- Paul Quinton (College of Policing)
- Professor Nick Fyfe (University of Dundee)
- Professor Jennifer Brown (LSE)
- Charlotte E. Gill (George Mason University)

Dedications

Sam Poyser

For Chris, Beth, Sonia and Graham, who have always believed in me; for Becky Milne, for her ongoing kindness and support; and for my brother Paul – possibly the best police officer in the world!.

Angus Nurse

To my nephew Connor, for asking all the right questions.

Rebecca Milne

For mum and dad, for all their support; for my mentor Ray Bull, for always being there; and for my son Sam, the superstar in my life.

Contents

List of abbreviations

ABE   Achieving Best Evidence
ACPO   Association of Chief Police Officers
CALA   Criminal Appeals Lawyers Association
CCRC   Criminal Cases Review Commission
CJA   Criminal Justice Act
CJS   Criminal Justice System
CPS   Crown Prosecution Service
ECHR   European Convention on Human Rights
ECtHR   European Court of Human Rights
FACT   Falsely Accused Carers and Teachers
FASO   False Allegations Support Organisation
HMIC   Her Majesty's Inspectorate of Constabulary
ICCPR   International Covenant on Civil and Political Rights
INUK   Innocence Network UK
IPCC   Independent Police Complaints Commission
IRA   Irish Republican Army
JENGbA   Joint Enterprise Not Guilty by Association
MIM   Murder Investigation Manual
MJSS   Miscarriage of Justice Support Service
MOJO   Miscarriage of Justice Organisation
MOJUK   Miscarriage of Justice UK
PACE   Police and Criminal Evidence Act
PAFAA/   People Against False Accusations of Abuse/
  SOFAP   Support Organisation for Falsely Accused People
PEACE   Planning and Preparation; Engage and Explain;
                 Account; Closure; Evaluation
PIP   Professionalising Investigation Programme
PTSD   Post-Traumatic Stress Disorder
RCCJ   Royal Commission on Criminal Justice
RCCP   Royal Commission on Criminal Procedure

About the authors

Dr Sam Poyser is a Senior Lecturer in Criminology, Criminal Justice and Policing at York St John University. After graduating from the University of Portsmouth with an MSc in Criminal Justice Studies (with Distinction), Sam went on to complete a PhD in Criminology, which examined the role of the media in investigating miscarriages of justice in England and Wales. A major element of this research compared the investigative attributes, skills and training utilised by investigative journalists to those used by senior investigating officers in the police. Sam has acted as an expert adviser to the BBC on the topic of miscarriages of justice and has liaised with journalists worldwide relating to stories in this area. She has also delivered training to pre-service and in-service police officers in a variety of areas, including critical failures in criminal investigation. Sam has published widely on the topic of miscarriages of justice, most particularly on the relationship between police investigation and miscarriages of justice.

Dr Angus Nurse is Associate Professor of Environmental Justice at Middlesex University School of Law, where he teaches and researches criminology and law. Angus has research interests in criminality, critical criminal justice, animal and human rights law, anti-social behaviour, and green criminology. He is particularly interested in animal law and its enforcement and the reasons why people commit environmental crimes and crimes against animals. Angus is a member of the Wild Animal Welfare Committee (WAWC) and has previously worked in the environmental non-governmental organisation (NGO) field and as an investigator for the Local Government Ombudsman. His books include *Policing wildlife* (Palgrave Macmillan, 2015) and *Animal harm: Perspectives on why people harm and kill animals* (Ashgate, 2013).

Professor Rebecca Milne is a Professor of Forensic Psychology at the Institute of Criminal Justice Studies, University of Portsmouth. The main focus of her work over the past 20 years has concerned the examination of police interviewing and investigation. Jointly with practitioners, she has helped to develop procedures that improve the quality of interviews of witnesses, victims and suspects of crime. This body of work has seen successful outcomes of the interplay between academic research and practical policing by coming up with solutions to real-world problems. As a result, she works closely with the police (and other criminal justice organisations), creating novel interview techniques, developing training, running interview courses and providing case advice. She is also the Director of the Centre of Forensic Interviewing, which is an internationally recognised centre of excellence for investigative interviewing that brings together research, teaching and innovation activities.

Series preface

The Key Themes in Policing series aims to support the growing number of policing modules on both undergraduate and postgraduate courses, as well as contribute to the development of policing professionals, both those new in service and existing practitioners. It also seeks to respond to the call for evidence-based policing led by organisations such as the College of Policing in England and Wales. By producing a range of high-quality, research-informed texts on important areas of policing, contributions to the series support and inform both professional and academic policing curriculums.

Representing the fourth text in the series, Sam Poyser, Angus Nurse and Becky Milne address the important issue of miscarriages of justice. This is a subject that received substantial media interest in the 1970s, '80s and '90s and has recently re-emerged as a pressing issue for criminal justice professionals and policy makers. This book is a crucial addition to the series because of the importance of miscarriages of justice and the lack of up-to-date texts on this subject. In policing, the theme of miscarriage of justice has historically been associated with police wrongdoing, cutting corners and bad practice. While these themes persist in some cases that go wrong there are also concerns around the reliability of forensic evidence, disclosure, the significance of technology, the reduction in legal aid and the reduction of budgets for the CPS and the police. *Miscarriages of justice* is not just about ethical concerns but also the reliability of the criminal justice system in an increasingly complex justice environment with fewer resources.

The three authors collectively provide a wealth of knowledge in miscarriages of justice and the media, law, and police investigation. This text not only provides an up-to-date account of miscarriages of justice but also provides insight into definitions, history, sources and remedies. This book will provide an excellent insight and a comprehensive account of the dangers and challenges of miscarriages of justice, suitable for criminal justice practitioners and students exploring the challenges of delivering effective criminal justice.

ONE

Introduction – what is a miscarriage of justice?

Sam Poyser

Introduction

In 2015, Eric Allison, a journalist who has investigated numerous miscarriages of justice in England and Wales, stated: 'I am convinced that there are more miscarriages of justice now, than at any time since I have been a student of the system – a study going back over half a century' (Allison, 2015). Despite such statements, we do not, indeed cannot, know the true scale of the miscarriage of justice problem because most cases are not the subject of appeal, or exposed by any other means (Belloni and Hodgson, 2000). What we do know is that miscarriages of justice have occurred throughout history and in all countries, and that they will continue to do so (Huff and Killias, 2013). We can never entirely eliminate them from the Criminal Justice System (CJS) because it is a system run by humans – and humans are fallible.

However, the latter does not mean that we have not successfully reduced the likelihood of certain factors being involved in the genesis of miscarriages of justice. For example, changes to policy, practice and legislation surrounding policing in England and Wales over the past 30 years or so have resulted in the improvement and professionalisation of techniques and standards relating to the interviewing of suspects. These have, in turn, reduced (what was in our not-too-distant history) a strong drive by police officers to *gain a confession* in the interview room and have meant that the interview process is now more likely to be viewed by officers as an opportunity to *gather information* (in the UK, see, for example, Clark and Milne, 2001). Such developments have, in turn, meant that miscarriages of justice linked to false *forced* confessions are not as common in the UK today as they once were (Gudjonsson, 2003). Nevertheless, other forms of false confession, such as those that are voluntary, continue to feature in miscarriages of justice. Indeed, recent research suggests that up to 20% of convicted criminals in England and Wales may have owned up to an offence that they did not commit (Townsend, 2011) and that young people and those with a mental illness and/or learning disability may be far more likely to volunteer false confessions than other groups, although mature adults of normal intelligence may also falsely confess (Gudjonsson et al, 2009).

Even if we have reduced the occurrence of *some* factors known to contribute to miscarriages of justice, the worrisome observation is that these may have been replaced with other 'new' factors that experts suggest will generate numerous miscarriages now and in the future. These include the raft of recent changes to criminal procedure and evidence that have made it easier to prosecute (Woffinden, 2010), such as the removal of fundamental safeguards for suspects, including the need for corroboration in some cases, and new approaches to hearsay, sexual history and bad character evidence (Newby, 2015). They also include major cuts to legal-aid funding for criminal appeals (Morris, 2015). The closure of the Forensic Science Service in 2012 and the shifting of testing onto the private sector and police forces has, many argue, resulted in fewer tests being conducted (due to the costs involved), standards dropping (Dodd, 2017) and forensic science now becoming more 'police-controlled' than ever before (Peachey, 2015). Additionally, the introduction of the Criminal Court Charge means that some innocent people quite literally cannot afford to plead 'not guilty' (Johnston, 2015)[1] and the introduction of fixed fees for solicitors preparing defence cases arguably disincentivises defence lawyers (McConville and Marsh, 2014). Such issues demonstrate something rarely mentioned in the miscarriages of justice literature, namely, that the factors involved in generating miscarriages are by no means *fixed*. Rather, they are *fluid* and dependent upon a whole variety of factors, not least human decision-making. Just as the decision-making involved in changes to criminal justice policy, practice and legislation can reduce the likelihood of particular forms of injustice, it can also pave the way for 'new' types of injustice to occur. Up to now, however, we have used the phrase '*miscarriage of justice*' without question. Before we proceed further, we must acknowledge various definitions of the term, and clarify what *we* mean when we use it within this book.

Defining miscarriages of justice

Defining exactly what a miscarriage of justice is can be difficult and, in some ways, depends upon our individual perspective (Quirk, 2007). While a lawyer, for example, may claim that a miscarriage only exists once a conviction is quashed (Naughton, 2005), a campaigner may argue that the CJS is imperfect in terms of recognising its mistakes and thus cannot guarantee that all wrongful convictions will be overturned (Morrell, 1999). The view of what a miscarriage of justice is may also depend upon what we consider the terms '*criminal justice*' and '*justice*' to mean. This requires consideration of the nature and purpose of the CJS and its relation to the notion of justice.

William Blackstone's (1858) statement that 'It is better that 10 guilty persons escape than one innocent suffer' forms the foundation of what Herbert Packer (1968) calls the 'due process' approach to criminal justice. This approach emphasises the presumption of innocence, individual rights and the protection of the individual from state power (Packer, 1968). Conversely, Packer's 'crime control' approach prioritises the forces of law (primarily the police) in being able to conduct their role of detecting the guilty without obstruction from excessive legal rules (Poyser, 2012). The UK is said to operate under a due process system, geared towards favouring the innocent. However, McBarnett's (1981) research examining 105 cases tried in Glaswegian courts highlighted very high conviction rates in this allegedly due process system. While acknowledging that the legal rules of the Scottish justice system differ slightly from those in England and Wales, this finding suggests that there is a gap between the *rhetoric* and the *reality* of the law (Eady, 2003).

In such a system, what is justice? Hall (1994) notes that where the state seeks to sanction an individual, the process is inherently coercive and unbalanced. Thus, it is the minimisation of these factors to tolerable levels that provides a limited but useful working definition of 'justice'. This suggests that 'justice' is determined as much by the integrity of the process (particularly by treating people fairly and respecting their rights) as by its end product (Walker, 1999). Arguably, many rights may be affected by the CJS in action. For example, as crime has an adverse effect on people's enjoyment of their rights, the CJS acts against offenders' rights so as to protect the rights of others (Walker, 1999). This said, how might the term '*miscarriage of justice*' be understood?

While many have highlighted inconsistencies inherent in defining a miscarriage (see, for example, Forst, 2004; Quirk, 2007), Walker (1999: 33) provides one of the most comprehensive definitions, arguing that just as 'justice' should be defined with respect to rights, so should 'miscarriages of justice':

> a miscarriage ... occurs whenever suspects ... defendants
> or convicts are treated by the State in breach of their rights,
> whether because of deficient processes or ... the laws

which are applied to them, or because there is no factual
justification for the applied treatment or punishment, or
whenever [such persons] ... are treated adversely by the
State to a disproportionate extent in comparison with the
need to protect the rights of others, or whenever the rights
of others are not effectively or proportionately protected
or vindicated by State action against wrongdoers or ... by
State law itself.

Evidently, then, a miscarriage of justice can occur not only within the
confines of the court system, but also when, for example: (1) police
unjustly exercise their powers on the street through gratuitous stop
and searches (Edmond, 2002); (2) arrests/detentions made do not
lead to charges (Greer, 1994); (3) there are failures in the application
of laws; and (4) injustice is institutionalised within laws (Belloni and
Hodgson, 2000).

Walker (1999) also argues that a conviction achieved through pre-trial
or trial practices that breach an individual's rights is a miscarriage, even
if they have actually committed the crime. This has been reiterated
in some judicial pronouncements, such as that of Lord Taylor, who
in quashing the murder convictions of the Cardiff Three in 1992,
declared that whether Stephen Miller's confession was true or not
was 'irrelevant' as it had been improperly obtained (Naughton, 2005:
172). Just as 'justice' is not only a 'result', but also a 'process', the
term 'miscarriage of justice' cannot be restricted to wrongful 'outcomes'
(Kennedy, 2004). Interestingly, Holmes (2002) distinguishes between a
'miscarriage of justice' and a 'wrongful conviction', stating that while
both terms refer to someone who has been illegally convicted, in the
former, the individual may or may not have committed the crime,
while in the latter, the person is factually innocent. However, in reality,
determining factual innocence is, of course, very difficult (Bedau and
Radelet, 1987).

Some of the problems evident in the preceding definitions are partly
due to the nature of the trial process itself, which is concerned not
with 'absolutes' such as 'innocence', but rather with pragmatics (Eady,
2003). For example, although the criminal justice process may claim to
attempt to uncover the truth about alleged offences, this is not done
at all costs. Prosecutors only have to produce a *sufficiency* of evidence
to establish 'guilt' (Edmond, 2002: 187). Similarly, as criminal appeals
test only whether convictions are '(un)safe', a quashed conviction is
an acknowledgement of a breach in the 'carriage of justice', *not* the

appellant's innocence (for further discussion and analysis, see Naughton, 2007).

Now we return to Walker's (1999) category of miscarriages, which arise through 'failure to vindicate the rights of others' (or, rather, victims). This is because, arguably, the concern of political (and, indeed, public and media) discourse has shifted during the last 20 years or so, away from the wrongful conviction of innocent and towards the wrongful acquittal of guilty defendants (Quirk, 2007). This is exemplified by a statement made in 2002 by the then Prime Minister Tony Blair: 'the biggest miscarriage of justice today is when the guilty walk away unpunished' (cited in Robins, 2011). Indeed, there are victims of *inaction* (such as the failure to properly investigate a crime) as much as there are of *actions* that lead to a miscarriage (Savage et al, 2007). This more recent focus upon victims and their place within the CJS demonstrates how cultural, social and political change can literally alter one's perception, and thus definition, of a 'miscarriage of justice'.

Importantly, how miscarriages of justice are defined affects estimates of their extent. The Criminal Cases Review Commission (CCRC, 2012) admits that it cannot always refer cases to appeal that, after analysis, seem to constitute a wrongful conviction. Additionally, it does not consider others worthy of investigation. Thus, the currently 419 convictions quashed on referral to the Court of Appeal, out of a total of 22,544 applications made to the body since its inception in 1997 (CCRC, 2017a), arguably amount to a conservative estimate of the number of people wrongly convicted since that time. Some victims may never fulfil the criteria of the appeals system and will never be able to overturn their convictions (Naughton, 2006). However, thus far, we have been concerned with wrongful convictions obtained in the Crown Court (Hall, 1994). Magistrates' courts, which deal with 98% of criminal cases, are the sites of numerous miscarriages (Ewick, 2009). Such miscarriages often go unnoticed as individuals may never appeal, perhaps because their sentence was not perceived as severe (Naughton, 2003). There are also impediments to defendants continuing to maintain their innocence, including the acts of charge, plea and sentence bargaining (Sanders et al, 2010). Indeed, research has found that deals offered by prosecutors may induce innocent people to plead guilty to crimes (Baldwin and McConville, 1979) and that many defence practices fail to act in a client-centred way, often being geared 'towards the routine production of guilty pleas' (McConville et al, 1994: 71; McConville and Marsh, 2014).

Clearly, the term 'miscarriage of justice' may be interpreted in different ways.[2] In this book, we primarily use the term to refer to wrongful conviction; however, there are clearly numerous complexities involved in this area and further debate is required.

Scholarly interest in miscarriages of justice

Scholarly interest in miscarriages of justice has increased massively over the past decade or so (Naughton, 2013). The first substantial study in this area was published by Borchard in 1932. This detailed 65 miscarriages of justice (62 US and three UK cases) and, crucially, forced a change in academic thought on the issue, from questioning whether miscarriages *do* occur, to a consideration of *why* they occur (ie what causes them) and how we can reduce them. Borchard's (1932) research revealed that the main causes of miscarriages were: (1) mistaken eyewitness identification: (2) improperly obtained confessions; (3) unreliable forensic science and expert evidence; (4) witness perjury; (5) inadequate defence representation; and (6) public pressure to solve horrific crimes. These findings were reflected in many subsequent studies, most of which were relatively small-scale (see, eg, Frank and Frank, 1957; Radin, 1964; Huff et al, 1986). However, this changed with the publication in 1987 of Bedau and Radelet's large-scale study of 350 miscarriages in US capital cases (from 1900 to 1985), which demonstrated that miscarriages were not the rarity once thought.

From the mid-1990s onwards, research in this field in the US permanently altered in nature. A study by Connors et al in 1996 triggered this change. This evidenced the ability of DNA testing to conclusively establish the prisoner's innocence in 28 individual cases. Subsequent research (Leo and Ofshe, 2001; Drizin and Leo, 2004), together with an ongoing database of DNA exonerations (Innocence Project, no date), in part, spurred a series of enquiries into the legitimacy of the death penalty in several US states (Leverick and Chalmers, 2014).

Miscarriages of justice research in the UK over the past decade has contributed greatly to the scholarly analysis of miscarriages, with some work showing promise in terms of meeting Leo's (2010) call for the development of *theories* of miscarriages (see, eg, Naughton, 2013; Jenkins, 2014). UK research has also helped to reduce some of the causes of miscarriages, particularly those linked to, for example, police interviewing (as mentioned earlier), investigative decision-making and suspect identification procedures (for a summary, see Poyser and Grieve, forthcoming).

The preoccupation of research with analysis of the causes of miscarriages is understandable as reducing their occurrence must be a priority. However, until relatively recently, miscarriages research had somewhat stagnated upon this issue. More recent research is breaking free from this focus in studying the *impacts* of miscarriages of justice. This scholarly endeavour is concerned with 'macro-level' consequences of miscarriages upon society and the CJS itself (see Cole, 2009; Gould and Leo, 2010) or 'micro-level' consequences of miscarriages for individuals who suffer them directly (see Grounds, 2004; Jenkins, 2013a). It also attempts to produce recommendations around how we might better respond to those consequences. Some of the studies conducted, and in progress, at the micro-level (see Jenkins, 2014; Hall et al, 2016; Poyser, 2016; Burtt, forthcoming) have benefitted from the fact that researchers have begun to forge stronger networks with campaigning organisations and similar groups. This has, in turn, provided them with access to willing research participants, many of whom desire to voice their experiences. Additionally, recent changes to the rules surrounding compensation awards for victims of miscarriages in the UK, which have resulted in most being ineligible for payment (Bartholomew, 2015), have no doubt added an additional urgency to calls for research into the consequences of miscarriages. Interest in miscarriages of justice on the part of scholars, students and practitioners continues to grow. It is an interest that this book aims to go some way towards furthering.

Aims and overview of this book

This book introduces the study of miscarriages of justice. The importance of this topic to practitioners working within the CJS and students of criminology, criminal justice and policing is undeniable, not least because miscarriages can provide 'lessons to be learnt'. In understanding how things can go wrong in individual cases, we necessarily have to also consider the opposite scenario, namely, how the CJS *should* work. Despite the obvious importance of the topic of miscarriages, there is a dearth of publications in this area worldwide. Focusing primarily on England and Wales, this book aims to go some way towards filling this gap. In doing so, it provides a comprehensive overview of some of the main topics relating to miscarriages of justice and of some of the most recently researched issues. With reference to a number of historical and contemporary cases, the chapters in this book, taken as a whole, demonstrate that despite policy, practice and legislative reform, miscarriages of justice remain a persistent problem, thereby reinforcing the notion that we must continue to seek to minimise them.

This chapter has attempted to define what a 'miscarriage of justice' is and introduced readers to an overview of scholarly research on the topic. It has demonstrated that providing a definition of a miscarriage of justice is complicated as denotations are influenced by a variety of factors, all of which can, in turn, be affected by cultural, social and political change. The chapter has also highlighted that definitions of a 'miscarriage of justice' may depend upon what we consider the terms 'criminal justice' and 'justice' to mean. With this in mind, the nature and purpose of the CJS and its relation to the notion of justice were briefly considered. An issue highlighted was the fact that, contrary to popular belief, the notion of 'innocence' sits uncomfortably alongside the notion of a miscarriage of justice. We also considered the contention that miscarriages of justice may be viewed as situations in which an individual's rights have been breached, regardless of their guilt or innocence, and regardless of whether they are suspect, witness or victim. This said, we noted that this book focuses primarily upon miscarriages of justice as wrongful convictions.

In focusing upon miscarriages of justice *as* wrongful convictions, Chapter Two, 'A historical overview of key cases' by Sam Poyser, explains that the latter have been an enduring feature of all legal systems since their inception but that we have, over time, become more aware of them, in part, due to media coverage/exposure of high-profile cases. The chapter examines examples of miscarriages of justice from the early 1900s through to more recent cases, primarily addressing those that, in themselves, exemplified problematic aspects of the CJS at particular moments in time and that were linked to four important criminal justice reforms in England and Wales. These are: (1) cases from the late 1800s/early 1900s and their relationship to the establishment of a Court of Appeal; (2) cases from the mid–1900s and their relationship to the repeal of capital punishment; (3) cases from the 1970s, particularly one relating to the introduction of the Police and Criminal Evidence Act 1984 (PACE); and (4) cases from the late 1980s/early 1990s and their relationship to the establishment of the CCRC. These wrongful convictions highlighted some of the most prominent causes of miscarriages and their devastating consequences. This said, disentangling such causes is no easy task.

As Chapter Three, 'The causes of miscarriages of justice' by Angus Nurse, demonstrates, a single miscarriage of justice usually has multiple causes, starting from an individual's first contact with the police and continuing to the end of their dealings with the CJS, when problems are not readily recognised and rectified by appellate mechanisms. Many of the causes discussed in this chapter are similar across different countries and time periods. Indeed, most of those revealed in early studies – such as poor defence preparation, non-disclosure, faulty forensic/expert evidence and the inappropriate use of laws – remain evident in successful appeals today. In 1948, Morgan, writing about the law governing evidence and trial procedure, stated:

> Our system does not guarantee either the conviction of the guilty or the acquittal of the innocent … [what it only] guarantees is a fair trial … a price which every member of a civilised community must pay for the erection … of machinery for administering justice, that he may become the victim of its imperfect functioning. (Cited in Joughin and Morgan, 1948: vi)

Chapter Three demonstrates just how imperfect the CJS sometimes *is* in terms of its administration of justice and how it has performed, and continues, in some respects, to perform, unsatisfactorily.

An important discovery from research into the causes of miscarriages of justice is that those that occur most frequently are linked to processes and procedures involved in criminal investigation, such as unreliable confessions, reliance on circumstantial evidence, and non-disclosure (Stevens, 2010; Forst, 2013). Research conducted by psychiatrists and psychologists has made the biggest impact in terms of helping to explain such phenomena. Chapter Four, 'Criminal investigation and miscarriages of justice' by Sam Poyser and Rebecca Milne, highlights how this body of research has aided our comprehension of the causes connected to criminal investigation, spotlighting issues surrounding the investigative *process* generally and interview *practices and procedures* specifically. It further highlights official responses to research findings and improvements made in the UK that have resulted in changes to criminal justice policy and practice, and to some of the causes of miscarriages in the UK (and some other countries) being reduced. Chapter Four ends by calling for further research aimed at minimising such miscarriages.

Our knowledge of the causes of miscarriages of justice is far more advanced than our knowledge of the harms they engender. What we *do* know is that miscarriages are damaging to society and costly due to the financial burden of imprisoning the wrong people. Miscarriages also undermine citizens' support for the CJS. More importantly, however, they devastate the lives of those who directly experience them. Chapter Five, 'The victims of miscarriages of justice' by Sam Poyser, examines the experiences of these individuals and how they are psychologically, physically, behaviourally, emotionally and financially harmed. The chapter also assesses the impact of miscarriages upon a prisoner's family. A critical point made throughout is that the effects of one miscarriage of justice that occurs at one point in time are often still felt decades after its exposure. Despite the plethora of harms caused by miscarriages, particularly to the wrongly convicted, at present, state responsibility for these individuals ends when their conviction is quashed. This chapter concludes by calling for change in order for victims to achieve truly tangible justice.

As Chapter Six, 'Formal remedies' by Angus Nurse, highlights, another area in relation to which calls for change have been made relates to the formal mechanisms in place to reveal and rectify miscarriages of justice. Up until the early 1900s, there was limited scope for appeal against criminal conviction in England and Wales. Attempts to introduce an appellate court were strongly rejected until 1907, when in response to public outcry regarding a series of high-profile wrongful convictions, the Court of Appeal was finally established. However, the Court subsequently received much criticism of its role and performance, culminating in the early 1990s in calls for the creation of an independent, non-judicial body that, once the standard appeal channels had been exhausted, might still investigate alleged wrongful convictions and refer them back to appeal. In 1997, this institution, the CCRC, began its work. However, it too has been criticised, particularly in terms of its activities and decision-making, alongside claims that together with the Court of Appeal, it is by no means infallible in terms of recognising and righting miscarriages. Chapter Six discusses such issues and assesses the effectiveness of these formal remedies.

As Chapter Seven, 'Informal remedies' by Sam Poyser, explains, many of those campaigning in the area of miscarriages of justice, rather unsurprisingly, feel that formal remedies are fallible in terms of rectifying many wrongful convictions, resulting in some innocent individuals remaining unjustly imprisoned. In such cases, informal remedies available to victims (and their families) may become important. Informal remedies, then, are often the final resort for individuals who have been failed at every stage of the criminal justice process, including the appellate system. These individuals now become dependent upon the hard work of others in order to help overturn their conviction and/or support them through their ordeal. Those involved in providing informal remedies include campaigning organisations, Innocence projects, journalists (including citizen journalists) and other charitable projects. However, this chapter argues that the true success of informal remedies often lies within prisoners' families. They often act as the 'driving force' behind campaigns against miscarriages and influence other entities to get involved in the cases of their loved ones.

In Chapter Eight, 'Conclusion' by Angus Nurse, a summary of the book is offered, drawing out the major findings of, and recurrent themes running through, Chapters One to Seven. It also offers recommendations that are based upon the contributions of the authors. It would be incorrect to suggest that nothing has changed for the better since the early 1900s, when there was the absence of even a proper appellate system in England and Wales. However, there is still a long road ahead of us. In 2016, Robins stated that the 21st anniversary of the Birmingham Six 'serves as a powerful reminder of the fallibility of our justice system' (Robins, 2016a). With this in mind, Chapter Eight concludes that our hope for the future is not that miscarriages will be expunged from that system, but: that their occurrence will be minimised; that where they *do* occur, it will become more evident, more quickly; and that adequate measures are put in place to support those who have, nonetheless, suffered. This will not only help those who fall victim to a miscarriage of justice; it will also enhance public confidence in, and respect for, our CJS.

One of the overall messages of this book is that miscarriages of justice present critical lessons for policing. This is because while miscarriages usually have many causes, the links between policing and the phenomena are undeniable. Whether on a doorstep, in a police car, on the streets or in the custody suites, there is the possibility that the seeds of a miscarriage of justice will be sown. The nature of policing as a front-line, public-facing profession means that the possibility of contributing to causing one, whether through action or inaction, is ever present. There is a tendency to think of miscarriages of justice as a thing of the past. They are not and never will be. Thus, there is certainly no room for complacency and plenty for continued vigilance on the part of police officers of *all* ranks and, indeed, all those who work for, and alongside, the CJS.

Notes

[1] An innocent defendant may enter a plea of 'guilty' to avoid the risk of a more severe penalty. So, for example, in the Crown Court, a charge for a guilty plea at the time of writing starts at around £900 but rises to £1,200 if an individual pleads 'not guilty' but is convicted after a trial (Johnston, 2015).

[2] For further discussion relating to the definition of miscarriages of justice in relation to awards of compensation, see, for example, Lipscombe and Beard (2015), *R (Hallam and Nealon) v Secretary of State for Justice* [2016] EWCA Civ 355 and Chapter Six of this book.

TWO

A historical overview of key cases

Sam Poyser

Introduction

> There will always be cases of wrongful [conviction] … no matter how many emendations are made to any legal system. (Brandon and Davies, 1973: 256–8)

Miscarriages of justice have been an enduring feature of all legal systems since their inception. However, over time, we have become more aware of them, in part, due to periods of increased media coverage of, and in some cases exposure of, particularly onerous cases (Poyser, 2012). This has, in turn, had a major impact upon public confidence in the criminal justice system (CJS) and has acted as a driver in prompting official responses to the problem (Nobles and Schiff, 2009). Such responses have included reforms to criminal justice policy, practice and/or legislation (Poyser and Milne, 2015). The efficacy of these reforms is discussed in detail in Chapter Six. However, as Brandon and Davies (1973) note earlier, they have clearly not completely rid the CJS of wrongful convictions.

The focus in *this* chapter is upon specific cases that might be considered to have contributed at the very least to social thinking about miscarriages, with some playing a significant role in the history of criminal justice reform. A complete chronology of all such cases is impossible within the space constraints of this chapter. Therefore, the ensuing discussion focuses primarily on miscarriages relating to murder cases as it is the exposure of wrongful convictions in these cases that has arguably had the most influence in prompting criminal justice reform (Brandon and Davies, 1973).

The chapter primarily addresses key cases leading up to four important moments of criminal justice reform in England and Wales. First, cases from the late 1800s/early 1900s and their relationship to what was eventually to be the moment of the establishment of a Court of Appeal (Criminal Division) (hereinafter referred to simply as 'Court of Appeal') in 1907 are examined. Second, cases from the mid-1900s that might be seen to relate to the first legislative step towards the repeal of capital punishment in 1965 are outlined. Third, some particularly unsettling cases that occurred around the 1970s are mentioned. Particular focus is placed on one such case and its relationship to the introduction of formalised police codes of conduct and practice in 1984. Fourth, cases from the late 1980s/early 1990s associated with reform in terms of the establishment of the Criminal Cases Review Commission (CCRC) to examine alleged miscarriages are addressed.

Key historical cases and the establishment of the Court of Appeal

We believe that in our Courts ... innocent men never are convicted. (*The Times*, 1860, cited in McCartney and Roberts, 2012: 1336)

The Court of Appeal, which permits an individual convicted of a crime to appeal against his/her conviction (Sanders et al, 2010), is an institution taken for granted today. However, in terms of the history of the CJS in England and Wales, it is a relatively new addition. For centuries, there was no effective machinery for correcting mistakes in criminal trials (Woffinden, 1987). The Home Secretary had the power to grant a pardon to those deemed to have been wrongly convicted under the prerogative of mercy; however, many viewed this process as unsatisfactory (Pattenden, 1996). A Royal Commission in 1845 had criticised this procedure; however, over 40 Bills to introduce an appellate court had been strongly opposed in Parliament. This was perhaps due to a belief in the infallibility of the trial system, as outlined in 1853 by the then Home Secretary Lord Palmerston, who proclaimed that there had been no miscarriages of justice in this country (Radzinowicz and Hood, 1986). For some time, this view was shared by many judges, lawyers and sections of the press (McCartney and Roberts, 2012: 1336), as highlighted by *The Times* newspaper quoted earlier. Concern that this assertion was simply wrong drove 11 witnesses to address the issue before the Royal Commission on Capital Punishment in 1864 (Hostettler, 1992). Interestingly, however, only one of them, Sir Fitzroy Kelly QC, favoured the establishment of an appellate court. He argued that between 1802 and 1840, at least 42 people had been sentenced to death who had later been proved to be innocent and that an appellate court would greatly diminish such occurrences (Block and Hostettler, 1997: 66). However, it was to take another four decades before reform occurred.

The Court of Appeal was finally established in 1907 due to the impact of a series of key miscarriages exposed during the previous decade (Sanders et al, 2010). These cases attracted much media coverage and, in some instances, journalistic investigations (see Whittington-Egan, 2001). More importantly, they involved individuals whom many of the public and authoritative figures protested were innocent of the crimes for which they were convicted (Nobles and Schiff, 2000). However, what was it about these cases that finally propelled much-needed reform?

Florence Maybrick

Florence Maybrick was convicted in 1889 of the murder of her husband, James, and sentenced to death. This cause célèbre obsessed the public and media for months (Birch, 2014). Florence's trial, presided over by a judge showing signs of mental illness, was allegedly poorly conducted (Colquhoun, 2015). However, the true concern, in the public mind at least, was that Florence's *guilt* was doubted. Florence was said to have poisoned James with arsenic. However, the medical evidence was contradictory, particularly as it was not disputed that: (1) James had been ill for some time; (2) he had faith in the 'medicinal properties' of poisons (his house was filled with them); and (3) doctors visited him to administer poisonous concoctions before his death (Birch, 2014). At her trial, Florence argued, but could not prove, that she had given James arsenic-infused meat juice at *his* request (Ryan, 1977). Sealing her fate, however, was perhaps the fact that she, like her husband, had another lover (Colquhoun, 2014). In his summing up, the trial judge hinted that the infidelious injury that Florence had foisted upon James was enough to damn her. A guilty verdict was followed by public outcry, with many, including public figures such as newspaper editor W.T. Stead, arguing that Florence was to be hanged for adultery, not murder (Birch, 2014). The Home Secretary eventually commuted Florence's sentence to imprisonment; however, her conviction remained firmly in the public mind and contributed to calls for a formal appellate mechanism.

George Edalji

A case with similar public impact was the conviction (and sentencing to seven years' penal servitude) in 1903 of Birmingham solicitor George

Edalji. Edalji was convicted of the disembowelling and maiming of a number of horses, cattle and sheep in the village of Great Wryley, South Staffordshire, in what was termed the 'Staffordshire Ripper' case (Weaver, 2006). The case caused widespread public panic, particularly relating to concern that the offender would soon turn to attack women and children (Weaver, 2006: 18). There were no witnesses to the crimes or forensic evidence, and despite devoting many resources to the investigation, police initially failed to detect a culprit (Oldfield, 2010). George eventually came to police attention through a communication from the local Justice of the Peace, who disliked his father, and through mysterious letters they received identifying him as the culprit (Whittington-Egan, 2001). Edalji's arrest and conviction attracted intense pubic disquiet (Christian, 2013). The Home Office rejected several petitions for a free pardon for Edalji, who vehemently protested his innocence. This inspired a national campaign spearheaded by the writer Sir Arthur Conan Doyle, who dismantled the case in a series of newspaper articles (Weaver, 2006). Following a Home Office inquiry in 1907, Edalji received a pardon; however, this miscarriage left an unpleasant taste in the mouth of the public (Lahiri, 1998) and further underpinned calls for the establishment of a Court of Appeal.

Adolf Beck

Perhaps the most well-known miscarriage of justice from this era is that of Adolf Beck. Beck's case gained prominence because he was wrongly convicted on *two* occasions of defrauding women in cases of mistaken identity (Sims, 2012). In late 1895, Beck was standing at the door of his flat in London when he was approached by a woman who said 'Sir, I know you!' (Cathcart, 2004). She believed that Beck was the man whom she had met recently on the same street and who had subsequently swindled property from her. Soon, a succession of women who had suffered similarly came forward to pinpoint Beck from identification (ID) parades. In 1896, Beck was found guilty of 10 counts of obtaining by false pretences and theft, and was sentenced to seven years' penal servitude (Sims, 2012). Upon Beck's release from prison in early 1904, almost exactly the same circumstances befell him. Again, a woman identified him as the man who had recently swindled her, followed by more women coming forward to pinpoint him as the culprit of similar crimes (Naughton, 2013). In June 1904, Beck was once again found guilty of fraud. However, shortly after his conviction, a man calling himself John Smith defrauded two women in London and was apprehended. Due to other evidence that subsequently emerged, it was clear that this man had also committed the frauds for which Beck had been convicted. Beck was freed and eventually pardoned. The case garnered much public and media attention and led to a Court of Enquiry in 1904 (Coates, 2001). This detailed errors relating to the conduct of the ID parades in the case and urged the establishment of a formal appellate mechanism (Pattenden, 1996). The Court of Appeal was eventually set up under the Criminal Appeal Act 1907 (Nobles and Schiff, 2000). The Beck case also contributed to a revision of the codes of practice surrounding procedures for ID parades (Sims, 2012).[1]

Key historical cases and the abolition of capital punishment

> On that evidence, he is entitled to be acquitted. That will not help him now. He is dead. (Sidney Silverman MP discussing the hanging of Walter Rowland in 1947, cited in Morton, 2015: 1)

The establishment of an appellate court cooled the crisis of public confidence relating to the need to officially correct mistakes made by the CJS; however, the possibility of making the most irreversible error remained. The death penalty had been a core feature of the CJS in the UK from 650 AD (Hostettler, 2009). Support for capital punishment was underpinned by official statements of confidence that, as Sir David Maxwell Fyfe (Home Secretary) in 1963 asserted, anyone who thought an innocent man could be hanged 'was moving in the realms of fantasy' (cited in Block and Hostettler, 1997: 155). However, others raised significant doubts about the guilt of many who went to the gallows. These included Walter Rowland, who was hanged for murder in 1947. His conviction was shrouded in doubt surrounding identification evidence, non-disclosure by police officers and gaps in the prosecution case presented at trial (Woffinden, 1987).

It would, however, be some time before any action was taken to abolish the death penalty and, in the end, this was eventually precipitated by just three cases (Naughton, 2007). These cases captured the nation's attention and provided the necessary 'force' required to induce a public crisis of confidence in the continued validity of capital punishment (Hostettler, 2009). What was to become known as the 'Evans–Bentley–Ellis trichotomy' (Naughton, 2007), representing all that was wrong with capital punishment, stuck in the public mind, as will now be outlined.

Timothy Evans

Timothy Evans, a young, barely literate, Welsh man, was hanged for murder in March 1950 after the bodies of his wife, Beryl (who had been strangled and sexually assaulted), and baby daughter, Geraldine, were found at 10 Rillington Place, a house divided into several flats, in London (Kennedy, 1961). Evans confessed to both murders, it is believed under police pressure, but, as was normal procedure in capital cases, was indicted for only that of Geraldine (Woffinden, 1987). By the time of his trial, he had retracted his confession, arguing that John Christie, who lived in another flat in the house, was the murderer. However, he was found guilty and hanged.

In March 1953, Christie moved out of his flat. A new tenant moved in and discovered a woman's body concealed behind a wall. Police later discovered another five hidden bodies, including that of Christie's wife. All had been strangled and sexually assaulted (Eddleston, 2009). Christie confessed to these murders and to that of Beryl Evans, but not to that of Geraldine, and was hanged in July 1953 (Oates, 2013). Christie's trial contained numerous references to Timothy Evans, and within a day of it opening, MPs demanded an inquiry into Evans' conviction, chiefly because 'here are two murderers, *one is asked to believe*, [living] in the same house, killing in the same way, hiding bodies in the same place' (Howard League for Penal Reform, 1953, cited in Hostettler, 2009: 264, emphasis in original).

The Scott–Henderson inquiry in 1953 concluded that no miscarriage had occurred, a decision that MPs argued had ignored a mass of evidence to the contrary (Woffinden, 1987: 18). This sparked a series of publications exposing fallibilities in the police investigation into Evans, a campaign by *The Northern Echo* newspaper and the formation of the 'Timothy Evans Committee', calling for a public inquiry and free pardon for Evans (Kennedy, 1961). The subsequent Brabin Inquiry in 1966 concluded that Evans had murdered his wife, but that Christie had murdered Geraldine, a theory with little foundation (Woffinden, 1987: 27). However, importantly, it added that no jury could have convicted Evans if all the evidence now available had been presented at trial. On 18 October 1966, Evans was granted a free pardon. Although the CJS had survived the public criticism, it had almost certainly hanged an innocent man, and the public knew it.

Derek Bentley

A case that had similar public impact during this period was that of Derek Bentley. Bentley was hanged for murdering a policeman in January 1953, having been convicted under the law of joint enterprise (Hostettler, 2009). The decision to hang Bentley, when he was indisputably not directly guilty of any violence, had no weapon and was under arrest when the murder occurred, was what engaged public opinion. Additionally, 19-year-old Bentley had a mental age of around 11 (a fact not disclosed to the jury) (Paris, 1991).

In November 1952, Bentley and his co-defendant, Christopher Craig (aged 16), were interrupted in their attempt to rob a Croydon warehouse by police officers. Bentley was swiftly arrested; however, Craig produced a gun and shot and killed PC Sidney Miles. Other officers alleged that Bentley had urged Craig to shoot, saying 'Let him have it'; however, he denied knowledge of Craig having a gun and both boys denied that this had been said (Eddleston, 2009). At trial, Bentley and Craig were found guilty of murder. Craig, too young to be sentenced to death, was sentenced to be detained at His Majesty's pleasure. Bentley was sentenced to death. The Home Secretary, Sir David Maxwell Fyfe, refused to advise a reprieve despite massive public support for Bentley, expressed through petitions submitted to the Home Office and a demonstration outside the Houses of Parliament (Koestler, 1956).

Years later, Constable Pain, an officer at the scene of the crime, whose testimony was not used in court, stated that Bentley had never said 'Let him have it' (Hobbs, 1997), and after years of campaigning by his sister, Bentley's conviction was quashed on 30 July 1998 (Mills, 1992). It was ruled that the trial judge had failed to adequately put Bentley's defence before the jury in his summing up, most particularly, that he had not directed them to consider whether since Bentley was under arrest at the time of the murder, this affected his responsibility for it. These were the same grounds (phrased slightly differently) as those presented at Bentley's original appeal in 1953 (Eddleston, 2009: 144).

Ruth Ellis

Unlike the cases of Evans and Bentley, it is not disputed as to whether Ruth Ellis committed the murder for which she was hanged in July 1955. Still, many felt that she did not deserve to die. Therefore, it was the perceived unjustness of her fate that placed Ellis in the annals of miscarriage of justice history (Dyer, 2003). This case caused much public disquiet and contributed to the climate of widespread public sympathy for the circumstances of condemned individuals (Block and Hostettler, 1997). At her trial, Ruth admitted that she intended to shoot and kill her lover, David Blackly (Dyer, 2003). However, the circumstances surrounding the killing were what attracted public sympathy for her. She was a young woman with two young children.[2] Shortly before the murder, Ruth, who many allege was beaten by Blackly, had a miscarriage (which he may have caused) and appeared to be in an unstable mental state (Hancock, 1963). Her counsel wanted to argue provocation as a defence (making her guilty of manslaughter); however, such a defence was narrowly interpreted at the time and the trial judge insisted that the evidence did not support it (Dyer, 2003).

Before her execution, Ruth revealed in a meeting with her solicitor that her friend, Desmond Cussen, whom she had been with on the night in question, drove her to the crime scene and gave her the gun. However, a prison officer said that he had overheard Ellis saying that she had *asked* Cussen for the weapon. This detail was later to be critical to the then Home Secretary Lloyd George's decision not to reprieve Ellis. This case contributed to a view held by a large section of the public that this punishment should not be retained, and less than 10 years later, in 1964, a Bill was introduced into the House of Commons by MP Sidney Silverman that marked the beginning of its demise. The Murder (Abolition of the Death Penalty) Act 1965 ended capital punishment for a period of five years initially. It was permanently abolished on 18 December 1969, although it was still possible to be hanged for offences such as treason until January 1999. In 2002, capital punishment during wartime was also abolished in the UK (Hostettler, 2009: 266–7).

Key historical cases and the Police and Criminal Evidence Act 1984

> [H]anging is not the only way in which the law can take
> [a] life. (Sedley, 2011: 146)

The abolition of the death penalty was a major development in criminal justice history. However, as Sedley notes, for those wrongly convicted of a serious crime such as murder, the torture of being imprisoned for decades may also effectively steal their life. Once the most irreversible error of the CJS had been abolished, there was space to consider *why* individuals might be wrongly convicted in the first place. Early research worldwide was beginning to reveal that while miscarriages have numerous causes, police investigative and particularly interview processes often play a central role (Radin, 1964; Brandon and Davies, 1973). Such issues are discussed in detail in Chapter Four. Here, it is suffice to say that initial findings reinforced concerns that had existed for some time surrounding the relationship between the police coercion of suspects and false confessions made during custodial questioning (Naughton, 2007). While the Judges' Rules (conferred by the Kings Bench judges in the early 1900s) detailed the proper procedure for custodial questioning, they did little to prevent *some* suspects from being pressured in police stations because they were 'rules of practice' rather than 'rules of law' (Hostettler, 2009: 251). Calls for greater police accountability accompanied by long-standing allegations of malpractice in the interview situation were not met favourably by those in power (Naughton, 2007). In fact, in June 1972, the Criminal Law Revision Committee argued for the *abolition* of the Judges' Rules and fewer restrictions on the admissibility of confession evidence so as to be far 'less tender towards criminals' (cited in Price and Caplan, 1977: 124). The drive required for reform eventually came in the shape of public and political concern surrounding the wrongful convictions of three vulnerable youths for the murder of a man named Maxell Confait.

Before we examine this case, we must note that false confessions to murder made by vulnerable suspects featured in many miscarriages occurring during the same decade (the 1970s) as the 'Confait case'. However, the difference between these convictions and those relating to Confait was that they were not exposed as being *wrongful* until decades later. They include that of: (1) Andrew Evans, convicted in 1973, who falsely confessed and whose vulnerabilities included memory problems, confabulation and false-internalised belief (conviction quashed in 1997); (2) Stefan Kiszko, convicted in 1976, who confessed under police coercion and whose vulnerabilities included an excessive fear of police and possibly other undiagnosed psychiatric illnesses (conviction quashed in 1992); and (3) George Long, convicted solely on the basis of his false confession in 1979 and whose vulnerabilities related to long-term clinical depression (conviction quashed in 1995) (Gudjonsson, 2003: 439). Unlike these wrongful convictions, those in the Confait case *occurred* and, crucially, were *revealed* within a short period. Consequently, the errors made remained fresh in the public mind and provided the necessary force required to strengthen calls for reform relating to the custodial questioning process.

The Confait case: Colin Lattimore, Ronald Leighton and Ahmet Salih

On 22 April 1972, the body of Maxwell Confait was found at 27 Doggett Road, South London, by police who had been called to a fire there. Confait had been strangled. A day later, three youths were arrested in relation to arson incidents in the area. Within a few hours and in the absence of a solicitor, the boys had confessed to Confait's murder (Price and Caplan, 1977). Lattimore, aged 18, had an IQ of 66 and was illiterate. Leighton, aged 15, was of borderline intelligence and near-illiterate. Salih, aged 14, was of normal intelligence and spoke English as a second language (Gudjonsson, 2003: 170). At trial, despite having retracted their confessions, they were found guilty of arson, a crime for which Salih was given four years' imprisonment. Additionally, Leighton was found guilty of murder and detained at Her Majesty's pleasure and Lattimore was found guilty of manslaughter on the grounds of diminished responsibility and detained indefinitely under the Mental Health Act (Gudjonsson, 2003). Lattimore's father began a campaign against his conviction. This attracted much publicity and journalistic interest, culminating in the screening of an impactful TV programme 'Time for murder' in 1974 (Eddleston, 2009). In 1975, the Home Secretary Roy Jenkins sent the convictions back to the Court of Appeal, where they were quashed.

A subsequent inquiry into the case (RCCP, 1981; see also Chapter Four) found that the Judges' Rules had been breached in that the police had: (1) failed to inform the boys of their right to a solicitor before being interviewed; (2) interviewed two boys without a guardian/ parent present; (3) ignored Lattimore's learning disability; and (4) posed leading questions (Gudjonsson, 2003: 171). Fisher's concerns regarding the case were taken up by the subsequent Royal Commission on Criminal Procedure (RCCP, 1981), which ordered psychological research to be conducted into custodial questioning (see Chapter Four). The results of this research led to changes in legal provisions under the Police and Criminal Evidence Act 1984 (PACE) and its Codes of Practice (Home Office, 1985a, 1985b), the aim being to improve the reliability of evidence and suspects' rights. PACE *required* that suspects' interviews were tape-recorded and that suspects were informed of their right to free legal advice before interview. It also introduced the role of 'appropriate adult': a person, independent of the police, to act as an additional safeguard in interviews with vulnerable suspects (Sanders et al, 2010).

Price and Caplan (1977: 122) suggest that the Confait case 'shook the public out of a comfortable complacency in the law and the police', providing the hard evidence required to underpin claims that some suspects were subjected to police malpractice (Naughton, 2007). One may ponder how legislative history would have differed had the Confait miscarriages remained hidden until many years later (as occurred in the other cases mentioned). PACE would have probably taken much longer to materialise. Importantly, however, the reforms that PACE brought about did not eradicate miscarriages. Nor, in the short term at least, did they significantly change police behaviour (see Chapter Four).

Key historical cases and the Criminal Cases Review Commission

> The root of injustice is ... the obsessive pretence that mistakes are [always] corrected on appeal and that what cannot be corrected on appeal is not a mistake. (Sedley, 2011: 146)

Many miscarriages discussed in this final section occurred in the same decade as the Confait miscarriages; however, *they* were not exposed until the late 1980s/early 1990s. By this time, they had captured public attention and raised much disquiet concerning the reliability of the convictions in question. For many, this was accompanied by broader misgivings concerning the efficacy of the mechanism that was supposed to rectify them, namely, the appellate system.

It will be remembered that the Court of Appeal was established in response to cases in which seemingly *innocent* individuals had been wrongly convicted. Therefore, its role was widely assumed to be to rectify such wrongful convictions when they occurred. During the 1980s/early 1990s, however, it became clear that the existence of this mechanism did not necessarily mean that it worked as those who needed to use it might expect. Indeed, during this period (chiefly as a result of media investigations), cases had come to public attention involving individuals who, despite being felt by many (including powerful social figures) to be innocent, had their convictions upheld at appeal (see Poyser, 2012). Additionally, the system in place to *refer* cases to appeal was being questioned.

At this time, the referral system involved political input. The Home Secretary had powers to refer a case to the Court of Appeal for determination if they thought fit. Therefore, those protesting their innocence would petition them to refer their case (McCartney and Roberts, 2012). This political involvement in the CJS was discretionary and based on the Home Secretary's views on the case and the individual's innocence. The difficulties inherent in this were exposed in a 1980s' BBC TV series called 'Rough justice' (Poyser, 2012). This detailed cases of prisoners who, based on the evidence presented in the programmes, appeared to be innocent of the crime for which they had been convicted. Importantly, each individual had unsuccessfully petitioned the Home Office for referral to the Court of Appeal.

The first three 'Rough justice' programmes presented evidence that resulted in the Home Office referring the cases back to appeal and two (of the three) convictions being quashed. This included 'Jock' Russell's 1977 conviction for the murder of a woman who lived in his block of flats in Deptford (Young, 2015). Witnesses saw the killer, who forensic experts testified was right-handed, jump 31ft out of his victim's window before running away. Russell was left-handed, had broken both ankles relatively recently (making it unlikely that he could have jumped without injury) and had hair that did not match the handful found in the dead woman's hand. Russell had been refused leave to appeal by the Home Office; however, after the programme in 1983, his conviction was referred back to appeal and quashed (Young, 2015). Clearly, the Home Office referral process partly depended on pressure placed on the Home Secretary, not just on a case's merits (McCartney and Roberts, 2012).

However, there were actually two issues at work here. First, there were questions of whether there should be political input into decision-making on whether to refer a case to appeal and the seeming reluctance of the courts to accept such intervention. Second, there was the appellate courts' apparent reluctance to consider cases where appellants argued wrongful conviction on *factual error* grounds (ie that the individual is innocent), rather than on *technical or legal error* grounds (ie that an inappropriate sentence or judicial misdirection to the jury was given), despite its powers (under Section 9 of the Criminal Appeal Act 1907) to do so. Thus, it was argued that the court was self-limiting its role, being more concerned with the integrity of the criminal justice *process* than with claims of factual innocence (McCartney and Roberts, 2012: 1351). It was effectively restricting its approach to correcting miscarriages by focussing on *reviewing* them, rather than *rehearing* the facts of them. This did not help factually innocent appellants with no failures of technical or legal error issues to argue. Determining whether the appellant was factually innocent required deeper investigation than simply assessing the fairness of the original trial (McCartney and Roberts, 2012: 4–5). Fresh evidence had to be found to undermine the safety of their conviction. Lord Devlin had recognised this problem when, in 1976, he highlighted the need for an independent tribunal to examine claims of wrongful conviction (Devlin, 1976), an idea rejected by the Home Office on the grounds that this would undermine the Home Secretary's freedom to reach decisions and effectively function as a court above the Court of Appeal. Prompted by cases such as those revealed by 'Rough justice', the idea was again debated in the House of Commons in 1988. However, a motion to introduce such a body failed by 121 votes to 45 (McCartney and Roberts, 2012). Eventually, the drive required for reform came in the shape of extensive public, media and political concern surrounding the failure to *right* wrongful convictions in what became known as the 'Irish cases'.[3]

The Guildford Four and the Maguire Seven

In October 1974, five people were killed as a result of the latest in a string of terrorist attacks committed by the Irish Republican Army (IRA). Pubs in Guildford and Woolwich had been bombed. A man named Paul Hill was arrested and falsely confessed to the offences. He said that he had travelled to England with his friend Gerry Conlon and that they and another man, Patrick Armstrong, had planted the bombs. This led to a round-up of suspects, including Carole Richardson, the girlfriend of Armstrong (Eddleston, 2012a). The four individuals were convicted and given life sentences. Their first appeal in 1977 was heard after convicted IRA terrorists confessed to the bombings, saying that the four were not involved (McKee and Franey, 1988). The appeal failed. Subsequently, the case garnered much public and media interest and was the focus of a massive campaign supported by many influential figures (Conlon, 1994). After the four had spent another 12 years in prison protesting their innocence, the Home Secretary referred the case back to appeal on grounds relating to the fabrication of confession evidence and the non-disclosure of exculpatory evidence, and the convictions were quashed (Walker and McCartney, 2008).

The outcome of this appeal prompted reconsideration of another case involving individuals convicted of terrorism offences, the Maguire Seven (Kee, 1989). Members of the Maguire family had been arrested alongside a family friend as a result of Gerard Conlon allegedly telling the police that his aunt, Anne Maguire, had instructed him in bomb-making (Sedley, 2011). Anne, her husband, Patrick, her two younger sons, Vincent (aged 17) and Patrick (aged 14), her brother, William Smyth, her brother-in-law, Patrick 'Guiseppe' Conlon, and a family friend, Patrick O'Neill, were convicted in 1976 on the basis of forensic tests on some of them that appeared to show traces of nitro-glycerine – deemed to be evidence of handling explosives. Those who confessed later said that they were tortured into doing so (Conlon, 1994). A first appeal in 1977 was refused and the 'Seven' served their entire sentences before the Home Secretary referred the case to appeal again in 1991. The convictions were quashed on the basis of the non-disclosure of evidence and the discrediting of the forensic tests (Eddleston, 2012b). As with the Guildford Four, many questioned why this had taken so long when the appellate system was supposed to swiftly and effectively rectify miscarriages. A year later, the same question was posed about another group of people – the Birmingham Six.

The Birmingham Six

Paddy Hill, Hugh Callaghan, Richard McIlkenny, Gerald Hunter, William Power and Johnny Walker were convicted in 1975 for the IRA bombing of a Birmingham pub that killed 21 people (Mullin, 1990). At their trial in 1975, the prosecution submitted that forensic tests had revealed the presence of nitro-glycerine on some of the men's hands and confessions were signed by four of them (which they claimed had been beaten out of them). They were found guilty and sentenced to life (Hill, 1996). Their appeal in 1976 failed. In 1988, the then Home Secretary Douglas Hurd referred the case back to appeal due to doubts surrounding the reliability of the forensic tests and a statement from a former constable who said that he had witnessed the men being beaten in custody. Their appeal was again dismissed (Mullin, 1990). Media interest in the case mushroomed, culminating in a series of TV programmes produced by 'World in action' that presented the results of a reinvestigation into the case and an interview with a disguised man who admitted to planting the bombs (providing information about their location never before made public) (McKee and Franey, 1988). As a result of mounting public pressure, the Home Secretary referred the case to appeal in 1991. Here, evidence was presented that the confessions had been tampered with and that the forensic evidence was flawed – grounds almost identical to those presented in 1988. The convictions were quashed on 19 March 1991 (McCartney and Roberts, 2012). These miscarriages provided the hard evidence to demonstrate that the appellate system was not working in the way that many thought it should and helped to underpin calls for urgent change.[4]

On the day of the Birmingham Six's release from prison, the Home Secretary announced a Royal Commission on Criminal Justice (RCCJ). Chaired by Lord Runciman, the Commission reported in 1993 and recommended that a body, independent of the executive, be established to investigate alleged miscarriages and refer them to the

Court of Appeal (Hucklesby, 2009). A year later, the May Inquiry (May, 1994) into the Guildford miscarriage, the results of which presented a serious embarrassment to the government, police and appellate system, came to similar conclusions. The CCRC was subsequently established, beginning its work in early 1997. Once again, the exposure of specific cases of wrongful conviction had provided the proof required to drive through reform of the CJS (Naughton, 2013). The CCRC would put an end to home secretaries neglecting to use their powers to refer cases back to appeal and exasperation concerning the operation of the Court of Appeal. It had the power to examine claims of wrongful conviction afresh and conduct independent investigations to try to find fresh evidence.

Sadly, however, after just over a decade of operation, the CCRC itself began to be heavily criticised in relation to its ability to fulfil what many believe to be its function, namely, to successfully deal with factually innocent appellants (Woffinden, 2010). As has been stated, appellants relying on a claim of factual innocence, rather than legal or procedural error, face the difficulty of finding fresh evidence for an appeal. In this respect, the CCRC has been criticised for allegedly preferring to conduct desktop reviews of claims of wrongful conviction in order to try to find legal or procedural argument (perhaps due to restricted resources) (see also Chapter Seven), rather than do the legwork in 'going out and reinvestigating' cases in order to try to find fresh evidence (Robins, 2012). This has led to questions surrounding whether it is actually 'fit for purpose', linked to examples of long-running cases in which alleged innocent appellants have been unable to get their convictions through the CCRC and back to the Court of Appeal, still less get them quashed.[5] The CCRC has openly admitted to inadequately investigating some cases. In 2014, for example, it apologised for failing to order a crucial DNA test that eventually led to appellant Victor Nealon's release after 17 years of wrongful imprisonment (Robins, 2015a). Naughton (2013) argues that the CCRC is a failure because, like the Court of Appeal, it is reluctant to involve itself in innocence claims. However, McCartney and Roberts (2012) contend that if the CCRC *has*, like the appellate court, prioritised procedural and technical grounds of appeal over those of factual innocence, we must reform the appellate court's illiberal approach to fresh evidence (ie factual innocence) appeals, not abolish the CCRC (for further discussion, see Chapters Six and Seven). Clearly, according to some, gaps remain in terms of our response to the problem of how to right the wrongful conviction of innocent individuals.

Conclusion

Over the last 100 years or so, the UK has seen a number of reforms to the CJS made in response to particular miscarriages of justice that provided a strong evidence base for reform (Naughton, 2007: 109). Since the exposure of the cases that led to the establishment of the CCRC in the 1990s, many more miscarriages have come to light. However, the changes, if any, that they have prompted have not been on the scale discussed earlier. These include high-profile miscarriages in what became known as the 'cot death cases', involving mothers, such as Sally Clark and Angela Cannings, convicted of the murder of their babies in cases where faulty expert testimony played a role (see Batt, 2004; Cannings, 2006), as well as the 'shaken baby cases', involving parents, such as Kevin Callan (Callan, 1998), and other carers, such as Suzanne Holdsworth and Lorrain Harris, erroneously deemed by experts to have shaken babies in their care to death (Malone, 2012). Such cases led appellate judges to warn that 'Special caution is needed where expert opinion evidence is … fundamental to [a prosecution]', as today's 'orthodoxy' may become tomorrow's 'outdated learning' (Tibbetts, 2008). Similarly, the joint enterprise law, which, under certain circumstances, allows a jury to convict individuals on the periphery of a crime of the same offences as those who committed it, has also recently been pinpointed as a potential source of miscarriages (McClenaghan, 2014; Green and McGourlay, 2015). Indeed, a landmark ruling made by the Supreme Court (in the case of Ameed Jogee in 2015) that the law has been wrongly interpreted for over 30 years may result in changes to the way the law is applied in criminal cases (Allen, 2016).[6]

Clearly, miscarriages of justice remain very much a 21st-century problem. The history of key cases detailed in this chapter serves to illustrate that we *can* reform the CJS in response to knowledge gained even if those reforms, in and of themselves, are not always perfect.

Questions for further consideration

1. Miscarriages of justice have been a persistent features of all legal systems since their inception. Consider why this is the case and who is involved in creating miscarriages.

2. Although miscarriages of justice have always existed, we have become more aware of them over time. This is partly due to

increased media focus upon the issue. What other factors might have played a role in increasing our awareness of miscarriages?

3. Looking back over a history of key miscarriages of justice in the UK and to reforms that followed their exposure, what, in your view, are the major lessons learnt from the occurrence of miscarriages?

Notes

[1] For further reading on developments surrounding ID parades, see Poyser and Grieve (forthcoming).

[2] In this respect, her hanging was unusual as out of 145 women sentenced to death in the 20th century, only 14 were hanged – a reprieve rate of over 90% (Hostettler, 2009: 265).

[3] The Birmingham Six, Maguire Seven, Guildford Four and Judith Ward were Irish or had spent time in Ireland during the 1970s – a period when the Irish Republican Army (IRA) conducted a bombing campaign in the UK. They were all wrongly convicted of terrorism offences.

[4] See also the flood of successful appeals following the disbandment of the West Midlands Serious Crime Squad in 1989 (see Burrell, 1999), who had also investigated the Birmingham pub bombings.

[5] See, for example, the case of Eddie Gilfoyle (Eddiegilfoyle, no date).

[6] Although see also Richardson (2016), who argues that the change may make little difference.

THREE

The causes of miscarriages of justice

Angus Nurse

Introduction

As the first few chapters of this book identify, providing a definition of miscarriages of justice is problematic. So, too, is identifying the causes of miscarriages of justice. In adopting the definition of wrongful conviction outlined in earlier chapters for this book's discussion of miscarriages of justice, this chapter identifies that a single miscarriage of justice can have multiple causes. Miscarriages of justice issues can start from an individual's first contact with the police, continuing to the end of their dealings with the criminal justice system (CJS), when potentially problematic judgments are not readily rectified by appellate or informal mechanisms (see Chapters Six and Seven). The term 'wrongful conviction' covers a multitude of issues, from failure in investigation through to errors at trial. Such errors can result in a conviction that may well be technically correct in the sense of having convicted the guilty party, but that may nevertheless have been achieved in a manner that cannot be considered safe, according to legal definitions (see Chapter Six). Accordingly, the discussion of wrongful conviction needs to extend beyond merely considering conviction of the innocent. It must also include examination of those cases where doubts exist about whether due process was followed, about evidential validity or about the manner in which evidence was collected. It must also consider doubts about the conduct of investigatory officers, experts and witnesses at trial.

Disentangling the causes of miscarriages of justice is difficult; however, this chapter examines a range of issues that have been thought to cause a miscarriage. Many of the causes to be discussed in this chapter are similar across different countries and time periods, including: poor defence preparation; the non-disclosure of evidence; the reduction in legal aid funding; the inappropriate use of laws, such as the joint enterprise law; and issues surrounding expert witnesses and forensic evidence. However, a miscarriage often has more than one cause and can reflect a situation where various errors, whether large or small, can result in a conviction whose safety can be questioned.

Cognitive bias: the citizen versus the state

In his foreword to the 2012 *Justice Gap* publication *Wrongly accused*, which explored responsibility for investigating miscarriages of justice, Mr Justice Sweeney said that 'our system of criminal justice is not perfect. Despite all its safeguards and the strivings of the vast majority of those of us who are involved in its conduct, a risk of miscarriages remains' (cited in Robins, 2012: 2). Where such miscarriages occur, it is important not only to identify that they have occurred, but also to ensure that society can uncover *why* they occurred and learn lessons to minimise future occurrence.

Many wrongful convictions arguably occur when the state, convinced that it has the 'right man/woman' directs its investigative and prosecutorial efforts towards constructing the case against the identified suspect(s). Investigative issues are considered in detail in Chapter Four and so are only briefly mentioned herein; however, the underlying nature of the adversarial justice system places the onus and evidentiary burden on the prosecution to prove its case beyond reasonable doubt. This arguably directs investigative resources towards proving guilt rather than uncovering truth, with the state's focus being on punishing the guilty. Indeed, Naughton (2011: 41) goes so far as to argue that the evidentiary burden and the nature of the adversarial system:

> places pressure on, and directs the bulk of the resources to, the police and prosecution to chip away at the presumed innocent status and construct cases from only incriminating evidence that might obtain a conviction, rendering innocent victims vulnerable to wrongful convictions.

In essence, CJS practices arguably fail in the aim of pursuing objective analysis of the facts in order to ensure 'the enforcement of the criminal law and the need to avoid the erroneous conviction of the innocent while ensuring the conviction of the guilty' (Law Commission, 1995: 4). Instead, criminal prosecution arguably focuses on a *selection* of the available evidence, that is, that which indicates an offender's guilt or that aids in the construction of a particular guilt narrative once an early investigative hypothesis has been formed (see Chapter Four).

Procedural problems, such as the non-disclosure of evidence, can also occur where the state's focus is on a particular case narrative and the selective use and discussion of evidence is deployed. Findlay (2012) suggests that adversarial systems (such as those of the UK and US) are marked by party control of the investigation and presentation of evidence. Accordingly:

> adversaries, each motivated by a desire to win (rather than a purely objective quest for the truth), search for evidence, present their versions of the evidence, and challenge the evidence presented by the adverse party while the judge and jury, as neutral decision-makers, play a passive role in receiving the evidence and then evaluating it to determine the truth. (Findlay, 2012: 913)

In one sense, the system arguably creates conflict – the police versus prosecutors versus the defence – with each 'side' pursuing its own objectives in order to achieve its own conception of a 'win'.

The criminal trial also risks being a mechanism through which the prosecution simply seeks to prove the defendant's guilt, with the odds distinctly stacked against the resources of the defendant when compared against the might of the state. Naughton's (2011) argument that the defence is often poorly resourced and is reliant on police and prosecutorial evidence that is unsuited to the task of defending against cases constructed in this way undoubtedly has merit, and points to disclosure issues and evidence handling as causes of procedural error. Yet, it would be too simplistic to place the blame for miscarriages of justice at the feet of well-meaning police officers or prosecutors who have made errors in case preparation or presentation. Instead, it can arguably be said that the very construction of an adversarial system that prioritises speedy justice over rigorous examination of facts in an effort to get to the truth is itself at fault. Rozenberg (1992) identifies how improper investigative practices by the police were identified as significant factors in historical miscarriage of justice cases according to evidence provided to the Royal Commission on Criminal Justice (RCCJ; the Runciman Commission), which published its report in 1993. The contemporary position has doubtless improved, and significant changes have been made in respect of UK policing practices and scrutiny mechanisms. In principle, the contemporary investigation process includes specific attempts to introduce objectivity, such as the Trace, Interview and Eliminate (TIE) strategy (College of Policing, 2017), which provides for the evaluation of suspects during an investigation. The Criminal Procedure and Investigation Act 1996 also specifies that when conducting an investigation, investigators should pursue all reasonable lines of inquiry, whether these point towards or away from the suspect (para 3.5 of the Act's Code of Practice). However, writers and campaigners like Robins (2012, 2017) and Eady and Price (2013) suggest that cognitive bias or a flawed investigative approach aimed primarily at determining guilt risk causing miscarriages via flaws in the investigation (see Chapter Four).

Investigative and procedural problems

Chapter Four identifies how historical investigative problems include the inappropriate use of laws and fabricated and unreliable confessions. Changes brought about by the Police and Criminal Evidence Act (PACE) (and its Codes of Practice) and in police interviewing practice have arguably lessened the prevalence of such problems in the UK, although in the US, confession-based interrogational practice and the risk of false confessions remain a concern (Walsh et al, 2016: 131). The contemporary reality is likely that there is not a widespread conspiracy among UK police officers to frame innocent men for crimes that they did not commit. However, miscarriages of justice, conforming to this book's definition of wrongful conviction, continue to occur (Naughton, 2007; Robins, 2012, 2017). Such miscarriages can often arise from a series of small mistakes that result from the certainty of criminal justice agencies that they have the right person (Leo and Drizin, 2010), influencing investigation, prosecution and the whole machinery of criminal justice, even where a suspect is innocent. The risk is that, inadvertently, evidence discovered after an initial hypothesis has been formed is not evaluated objectively and conflicting information might be ignored or remain undiscovered (Brookman and Innes, 2013; Fahsing, 2016; see also Chapter Four).

However, Article 6 of the European Convention on Human Rights (ECHR) guarantees the right to a fair trial and so is of relevance to discussions concerning miscarriages of justice causes. Stone (2010: 22) observes that Article 6 'has proved to be one of the most widely used of the Articles'. In addition to the requirements that trials should generally be public, Stone (2010: 22) notes that Article 6 also contains:

> some specific rules relating to those charged with criminal offences, such as the presumption of innocence, the right to clear information on the charges, the right to adequate

facilities to prepare a defence, the right to legal assistance, and the right to examine witnesses.

The Human Rights Act 1998 incorporates these elements into UK law, offering a potential remedy in respect of policing practices that are not human rights-compliant, and in a wider context, human rights provisions dictate that police decision-making must be 'reasonable' and compatible with ECHR rights. Yet, the selection of evidence to better suggest a defendant's guilt risks generating wrongful and 'unsafe' convictions (Etter, 2012), particularly where these may impact negatively on the human rights of a suspect and the fairness of the trial process (also see Chapter Six). Naughton (2012: 21) identifies that 'inherently unreliable forms of evidence are increasingly seen as admissible in criminal trials'. Indeed, the European Court of Human Rights (ECtHR) and domestic courts have ruled that illegally or unfairly obtained evidence will not always be excluded from trials, although fairness issues should be considered in deciding whether to admit evidence.[1] However, concerns about contemporary evidentiary issues are illustrated by a brief analysis of the causes for referral of cases to the Court of Appeal by the Criminal Cases Review Commission (CCRC) during 2015 and 2016. These identify a range of issues relating to possible problems in investigative and evidentiary processes, including: conduct of a police officer; failure to disclose evidence to the defence (several cases); evidence of alternative suspects; misinformation and poor advice about the strength of evidence against the accused (which resulted in a guilty plea); and flaws in expert evidence (CCRC, 2017b).

In a 2010 law research paper for the University of San Francisco, researchers Leo and Drizin identify that false confessors whose cases are not dismissed before trial are often convicted despite their innocence. Their analysis of US data concludes that once innocent individuals have been misclassified as guilty by police, the conduct of the CJS is entirely based around proving that guilt, beginning with a guilt-presumptive, accusatory interrogation. In part, this reflects the reality that once informed that an individual has confessed, juries may place undue weight on the confession evidence to the exclusion of other evidence (Leo and Ofshe, 1998: 429). Thus, as a cause of wrongful conviction, inappropriately obtained or false confessions are a significant cause in shaping the minds of jurors, particularly in respect of the common-sense notion that an innocent individual would not confess to a crime that they had not committed. The US evidence considered by Leo and Drizin indicated that once a false admission is obtained, pressure is often placed on the suspect to provide a post-admission narrative jointly shaped with investigators, who often supply the innocent suspect with the (public and non-public) facts of the crime, which further shapes their guilt. Leo and Drizin (2010) identify that poorly trained but confident police investigators can misclassify some innocent individuals as guilty. Once this has occurred, a narrative is constructed that establishes the innocent person's guilt on the basis of an unwavering (yet mistaken) presumption of guilt. This is then transferred onto prosecutors and judges, resulting in the conviction of the innocent party (see also Chapter Four). While such issues are arguably no longer as significant a problem in the UK as they once were given contemporary safeguards on interviewing and policing practice, the following case study illustrates how such narrative construction occurs.

Case study: The Cardiff Three

The Cardiff Three case relates to the investigation into the murder of Lynette White on 14 February 1988 and the associated wider miscarriage of justice issues that occurred in South Wales at the time of this case. Originally, five innocent men were arrested, charged and initially held in prison for White's murder. Three of the men were subsequently convicted and sentenced to life imprisonment, serving several years in prison before being released on appeal in 1992.

In 1988, White, a 20-year-old sex worker, was found dead with more than 50 stab wounds. Whereas the search was initially for a dark-haired white suspect, five young non-white men, Tony Paris, Yusef Abdullahi, Stephen Miller (White's boyfriend) and John and Ronnie Actie, were arrested and charged with her murder. In 1990, Paris, Abdullahi and Miller were convicted and jailed for life while the Acties were acquitted. Miller had admitted killing his girlfriend, allegedly after being interviewed 19 times over a period of four days. However, Michael Mansfield QC, representing Miller, notes that Miller had actually protested his innocence over 300 times during interviews (Campbell, 2012).

In 1991, journalists began to question the safety of the convictions, and media interest and a public campaign to overturn the convictions contributed towards the Cardiff Three being granted leave to appeal. An alibi witness for Miller who had not been called at the original trial was also uncovered. The convictions were quashed by the Court of Appeal in 1992. *The Cardiff Three* case identifies the existence (at that time) of the three sequential errors identified by Leo and Drizin (2010: 13): *misclassification, coercion* and *contamination*. Once *misclassified* as guilty, a hostile and intimidating approach was taken to the suspects, which, in one case, was described by Michael Mansfield QC as bullying a suspect with 'hectoring and demeaning questions until his insistent denials of involvement were worn down to submissive "confessions"' (coercion) (Sekar, 2013). The Court of Appeal concluded that Miller's confession had been extracted during problematic lengthy police interviews. The confession amounted to an oppressive interview, a breach of Section 76 of PACE.[2] Lord Chief Justice Taylor concluded that, 'Short of physical violence, it is hard to conceive of a more hostile and intimidating approach by officers to a suspect' (Campbell, 2012). Accordingly, the Court of Appeal accepted that the suspects had been bullied, threatened, abused and manipulated by the police into agreeing to a 'contaminated' account of events entirely constructed around the mistaken presumption of guilt.

South Wales Police commissioned an independent review of the first police investigation by two former senior police officers from Lancashire Constabulary. The Hacking and Thornley Review commissioned in 1999 identified serious failures by individual officers, as well as 'corporate failure' by South Wales Police senior management in failing to provide proper management and oversight of the original murder investigation. The Independent Police Complaints Commission (IPCC, 2013) concluded that Hacking and Thornley identified what they thought could be potential criminal actions and serious misconduct by officers working on the first investigation. They also identified areas of serious concern where key witness evidence changed in favour of the prosecution after the defendants had been either arrested and/or charged. Prosecution witnesses, complicit in constructing a guilty narrative, were eventually charged with perjury and, in their 2008 trial, claimed that they had been harassed into lying by the police. Mark Grommeck, Angela Psaila and Leanne Vilday were jailed (in 2008) after pleading guilty to giving perjured evidence in the case against the Cardiff Three in the two trials in 1990. The trial judge acknowledged that pressure had been put on them by the police officers investigating Lynette White's murder, stating that:

> it has been accepted by the prosecution and I, too, accept that you are to be sentenced on the basis that all three of you, vulnerable in different ways as you were, seriously hounded, bullied, threatened, abused and manipulated by the police during a period of several months leading up to late 1988, as a result of which you felt compelled to agree to the false accounts that they were suggesting to you. (IPCC, 2013)

The Cardiff Three case arguably illustrates evidentiary problems relating to the manipulation of evidence to construct an appropriate narrative, which, in this case, included a false confession and alleged malpractice via forcing witnesses to provide false testimony. Cognitive bias and pressure for results may result in premature closure of a case where the evidence is seemingly constructed to confirm a case hypothesis (see also Chapter Four). However, in the Cardiff Three case, the availability of new DNA technology allowed forensic scientists to construct a fresh crime scene DNA profile, which led to Jeffrey Gafoor in 2002. In 2003, Gafoor confessed to White's murder and was sentenced to life imprisonment (Bennetto, 2003). The evidence on which Gafoor was convicted demonstrated that the witnesses in the original case gave incorrect evidence and also suggested that there were serious shortcomings in the police investigation.[3]

Investigative and evidentiary issues potentially impact on the extent to which a suspect is able to effectively mount a defence. Yet, poor or ineffective representation that fails to address investigative shortcomings can also lead to miscarriages, as the following section discusses.

Representing the client

The criminal defence lawyer is both an essential part of preventing miscarriages of justice and, regrettably, a significant cause of many miscarriages. Poor representation of clients and a failure to properly scrutinise the police investigative process that has led to a presumption of their client's guilt are major factors in allowing errors by the state to result in flawed convictions. Lawyer Maslen Merchant (2011) argues that 'today's criminal lawyer is a businessman first and foremost' and that many lawyers fail their clients by prioritising business over proper representation. Merchant identifies a range of factors impacting the ability of criminal lawyers to defend their clients effectively. Some are internal, others are external. Yet, the effect of flaws in either the prosecution's or defence's investigation of the evidence is often the same: the state gains a conviction even where evidence may exist to prove the defendant's innocence.

The United Nations' (UN's) Havana Declaration, which relates to the role of lawyers, identifies that all defendants 'are entitled to call upon the assistance of a lawyer of their choice to protect and establish their rights and to defend them in all stages of criminal proceedings' (Office of the High Commissioner for Human Rights, 1990). Article 6 of the ECHR broadly replicates this provision (see Chapter Six). Article 6(3)(c) provides that everyone charged with a criminal offence has, as a *minimum*, the right to defend themselves in person or through legal assistance of their own choosing or, if they have not sufficient means to pay for legal assistance, to be given it free when the interests of justice so require. The ECtHR has held that the right of access to justice must be practical and effective, not theoretical and illusory. In

Airey v Ireland [1979] (Application No. 6289/73), [1979] ECHR 3, (1980) 2 EHRR 305, the ECtHR concluded that the right of effective access to the court may entail a right to legal aid. The ECtHR has also determined that the 'interests of justice' may dictate that legal aid should be provided, particularly where the complexity of the case, the ability of the accused to represent themselves and the seriousness of any sanction (eg deprivation of liberty) are factors.[4]

The case law of the ECtHR and domestic law such as PACE also reinforces the right to a lawyer to defend and uphold a suspect's rights. The ECtHR has also held that the right to be *effectively* defended by a lawyer arises at the investigative stage.[5] Thus, from a very early stage in proceedings, the ability of the defence lawyer to effectively investigate the case against their client and to challenge flaws in the state's reasoning through effective representation are vital to uncovering miscarriages and preventing wrongful convictions. However, the Criminal Procedure Rules, recent cuts in legal aid in England and Wales, and a range of other factors have substantially impacted on the role of the defence lawyer, to the extent that lawyers may be unable to effectively fund the full range of investigative inquiries required to identify a potential miscarriage of justice during the process of a case. The decision on whether to commission expert reports, for example, psychiatric reports, or forensic experts will obviously need to be taken on a case-by-case basis. The UN Declaration, Article 6 of the ECHR and the realities of how miscarriages occur mean that this duty is firmly placed on the criminal lawyer from the point at which their client is charged and throughout the investigative and prosecution process. Thus, identifying a miscarriage is not solely an issue for the lawyer to pursue by way of appeal or referral to the CCRC after conviction; rather, it is an active issue to be considered during a defence. However, many lawyers fail in this task; some by virtue of poor work on behalf of their client, and others as a result of the confines of the legal aid system and business practices that are focused too heavily on providing an *expedient* defence rather than the best defence required for the case (Merchant, 2011; Nurse, 2012). Merchant (2011) goes so far as to suggest that a very high proportion of wrongful convictions are the fault of poor defence work by lawyers, and that some solicitors now do little more than read the prosecution evidence, have a cursory appointment with the client and nothing else.

In *R (Adams) v Secretary of State* [2009] EWHC 156 (Admin), Mr Adams was convicted on 18 May 1993 of the murder of Jack Royal. His conviction was referred to the Court of Appeal in 2007 on the grounds that incompetent defence representation had deprived him of a fair trial. The claim was that his defence team had failed to consider unused material provided by the police that would have assisted in undermining the evidence given by the sole prosecution witness. In considering Adams's appeal, the Court of Appeal found that if this had been done, the jury might not have been satisfied of Mr Adams' guilt, although he would not inevitably have been acquitted.[6] Disclosure issues (and inadequate counsel) are discussed in more detail in the following section, although this example illustrates the importance of effective counsel during the trial process.

Preventing miscarriages: inadequate counsel and the disclosure of material

The best way to deal with a miscarriage of justice is to prevent it from happening in the first place. In *Goddi v Italy* [1984] (Application No. 8966/80), the ECtHR said that the courts must ensure that defendants have an opportunity for a fair trial, which includes an adequate defence. Defining what constitutes an adequate defence in the context of each case may be difficult to determine; yet, as a minimum, it should include effective scrutiny of the Crown's case and the evidence against the lawyer's client in order to be practical and effective. Should this extend to a full examination of *all* the evidence, including any unused material? Merchant (2011) argues that it should, identifying that arguments that can be used to derail the prosecution case are often found in the unused material. At a more fundamental level, it is the prosecution's role to present its case against the accused and the defence's role to examine the merits and validity of that case and identify where it is lacking. Doing so may require the use of a range of expertise, including dedicated investigators able to identify investigative or prosecutorial errors and to sift through the unused material to identify holes or alternate lines of enquiry not pursued. Yet, the extent to which extensive defence scrutiny of the case takes place is variable and can be a cause of miscarriage of justice even though a review of unused material may be a necessary step in cases where a miscarriage is suspected. The House of Lords, in *R v H and C* [2004] 2 AC 134, stated:

> Fairness ordinarily requires that any material held by the prosecution which weakens its case or strengthens that of the defendant, if not relied on as part of its formal case against the defendant, should be disclosed to the defence. Bitter experience has shown that miscarriages of justice may

occur where such material is withheld from disclosure. The golden rule is that full disclosure of such material should be made. (Para 47)

Yet, the evidence of recent cases is that the disclosure rules are not fully working and thus the onus rests on defence lawyers to conduct effective scrutiny and enforce disclosure where required. However, defence lawyers arguably cannot enforce the disclosure of material when they are unaware of its existence, and Merchant (2011) raises doubts that this is working effectively, stating that:

> Legal aid fees in the Crown Court are, basically, calculated taking into account the seriousness of the case, the page count of prosecution evidence and whether it is a guilty plea or how long the trial lasts. You get paid the same amount at the end of the case if you do 10 hours' or 100 hours' work. It follows, therefore, that the less work you do the higher your profit margin. The less work you do for your money the more cases you can do at any one time. There exists a positive financial disincentive to do the job properly, which is scandalous. It undermines the whole ethic of someone being rewarded for a job well done.

Kim Evans (2012) has also noted that unused material can run to thousands of pages and can be the perfect place to hide evidence that can undermine the prosecution case. This is not to suggest that material has been deliberately withheld by the prosecution; evidence that could support a defendant's case at trial might not be disclosed by the prosecution, but might equally be missed by the defence team:

> Unless you are a lawyer with a deep sense of justice, there is little motivation to plough through this material for no financial reward, and with many solicitors' firms laying off staff, there are fewer and fewer people available to do the work. (Evans, K., 2012)

Potentially, this is the crux of the problem. In the US, where the nature of the legal system and the free market economy that surrounds it are such that criminal defence can be a lucrative profession, defence investigators are an integral part of the system (Roberts, J., 2003). Defending a client requires not only assessing the legal arguments and preparing a legal defence, but also going beyond key prosecution documents and getting to grips with how the police investigation was conducted, how the evidence was obtained and where there are not only flaws in the basic case against a client, but also flaws in the investigative process that have led to a flawed or mistaken conclusion on a client's guilt. In essence, the UK's current system asks criminal defence lawyers to do this, but in the case of legal aid cases, it does not pay them adequately for doing so (Merchant, 2011; Evans, K., 2012). This not only creates a disincentive to carry out a thorough investigative review and provide an effective defence based on detailed understanding of the investigative process; it also creates reliance on the use of the (readily) available documents and materials supplied by the prosecution to construct a defence in the name of managerial efficiency. Where this happens, trials may become unfair in a context where the defence is unable to effectively contest an evidentiary narrative constructed by a state with greater resources at its disposal.

The courts, in *R v Birmingham and Others* [1992] Crim LR 117, have held that the prosecution's failure to disclose material may lead the courts to stay proceedings on grounds of abuse of process. However, a stay on proceedings would only be imposed where the defendant can show that they would suffer such prejudice that a fair trial would not be possible. Given the manner in which issues surrounding unused material are currently handled, which this chapter illustrates, this is potentially problematic for the defendant whose lawyer is unable to allocate significant investigatory resources to a case. Defence inability to examine evidence is also a factor that could give rise to problems according to the leading case of *R (Ebrahim) v Feltham Magistrates' Court; Mouat v DPP* [2001] 2 Cr App R 23, which concerned the non-availability of a video-recording alleged to have contained material relevant to the defence. The potential issue where there has been a breach of the obligation to obtain and/or retain material (under either the Criminal Procedure and Investigations Act [CPIA] 1996 Code of Practice or in the Attorney General's Guidelines on Disclosure) is that the onus rests on the *defence* to show, on a balance of probabilities, that the absence of the relevant material has caused serious prejudice to the defendant to the extent that a fair trial could not take place. In *Sofris v S* [2004] Crim LR 846, the ECtHR considered this issue and concluded that Article 6 of the ECHR (the right to a fair trial) would only be violated as a result of the destruction of evidence where the loss of evidence put the defendant at a disadvantage compared with the prosecution. The hurdles that a defendant faces in, first, knowing that this has happened and, second, having sufficient evidence to prove this to a court's satisfaction seem considerable. It would also be difficult after the conclusion of a trial to argue that an abuse had taken place of such significance that the proceedings should have been stayed. However, the Court of Appeal might be invited to treat evidence that has been withheld and that later comes to light as fresh evidence (for further discussion, see Chapter Six).

Trial problems: expert and forensic evidence

Problems may also occur at trial where procedural fault causes a jury to reach a decision that might be questionable or unsafe (see Chapter Six). Trial judges should 'exercise a more vigorous line in preventing cases from going to the jury where there is insufficient evidence to support a sound conviction or there has been what is called an abuse of process' (Zellick, 2010: 15). Yet, to a certain extent, once the Crown Prosecution Service (CPS) has decided to pursue a case and the appropriate information has been laid before the court, a trial is likely to proceed unless there are serious material errors that dictate otherwise. Thus, the task of identifying faults in or weighing evidence is largely reliant on effective jury scrutiny and understanding, and it is here where further miscarriages can occur.[7]

Expert witnesses can be called to assist the court in their deliberations, and one of the central questions on admissibility of expert evidence is whether it aids or detracts from the court's deliberations (Keane, 2006: 553). In essence, witnesses are able to give expert opinion in matters without which the jury's 'lack of skill or experience would leave it ignorant' (Keane, 2006: 553). They are also there to 'furnish the judge or jury with the necessary scientific criteria for testing the accuracy of their conclusions ... and to form their own independent judgment' (Keane, 2006: 553). Before an expert witness can give opinion evidence, the judge has to decide if they are an expert. What constitutes an expert covers a wide range of areas of knowledge. For example, in *R v Silverlock* [1894] 2 QB 766 opinion evidence from a solicitor was admitted regarding handwriting although he had only studied it as a hobby – that is, specific 'scientific' qualifications are not necessary and it is for the court to decide what constitutes expertise relevant to a case. Indeed, in *R v Abadom* [1983] 1 All ER 364, it was identified that a properly qualified expert is entitled to rely on what might otherwise be considered as hearsay (evidence that is normally inadmissible). Experts can thus report on findings by other experts in the same field in support of an opinion on any given set of facts where such evidence might otherwise not be introduced. This risks juries becoming confused about levels of expertise and the weight to be given to expert evidence. Potentially, the greater availability of expert evidence for the prosecution case puts the defence at a disadvantage.

Misleading statistical evidence presented by experts can account for miscarriages when juries place undue weight on evidence or are convinced by possibly misleading evidence. For example, in his trial evidence in *R v Clark (Sally)* [1999] (unreported), where the defendant was charged with killing her two infant sons, Sir Roy Meadow testified that the probability of there being two deaths from Sudden Infant Death Syndrome in one family was about 1 in 73 million. This figure was based on a report, *Sudden unexpected deaths in infancy*, subsequently published by the Stationery Office (Fleming, P., 2000). Clark was convicted in November 1999 and her convictions were upheld at appeal in October 2000 but subsequently overturned following a second appeal in January 2003. At the second appeal, evidence was submitted that the prosecutor's pathologist had failed to disclose microbiological reports which suggested that one of her sons had died of natural causes. Thus, in one sense, the case illustrates disclosure failure as a cause of miscarriages. Meadow's evidence was widely considered to be a determining factor in Clark's conviction. However, his statistic was the subject of a *British Medical Journal* editorial, 'Conviction by mathematical error?' (*BMJ*, 2000), which said that the 1 in 73 million figure was seriously flawed and that the odds of the same family having two cases of cot death were much lower, at 1 in 8500. Thompson and Shumann (1987) coined the term 'The Prosecutor's Fallacy' to describe such a situation where the prior probability of a random match is assumed to be equal to the probability that the defendant is innocent. While in *R v Clark*, it appears that a statistical error was at issue; cases where statistical evidence provides a misleading and inflated suggestion of guilt also account for miscarriages (Matthews, 2004; Head and Mann, 2009: 534). Juries may also be confused by apparently conflicting evidence, particularly where experts can and do disagree on the 'correct' interpretation of evidence. The following case study illustrates this.

Case study: *R v Jenkins (Siôn David Charles)* 98/4720/W3

On 15 February 1997, Billie-Jo Jenkins was found murdered, having been battered over the head at least 10 times with an iron tent peg while painting patio doors at her family's home in Hastings, East Sussex. Her foster-father, Siôn Jenkins, was charged and eventually convicted of the murder but has always maintained his innocence and was eventually acquitted.

Both prosecution and defence agree that Billie-Jo was bludgeoned to death. Siôn Jenkins says that she was found lying on the patio, facing away from the house and broadly parallel to it, her legs straight out. There was thick blood all around her head and the left side of her face was against the patio concrete. The autopsy concluded that the cause of death was head injury caused by repeated blows to the head. There were 20 main injuries altogether, with seven large areas of laceration to the head. The skull had been fractured and brain tissue was exposed.

The prosecution argued that Siôn Jenkins had returned to the house in the afternoon of Saturday 15 February 1997 with two of his daughters, Annie and Lottie, and entered where Billie-Jo had been painting the patio doors. Then, in an uncontrollable rage he bludgeoned her to death. He then took his two daughters out to a DIY store in order to create a false alibi for himself. On their return to the house, he found the body and called 999 for help.

During proceedings, Siôn Jenkins acknowledged being at the scene and touching the body, possibly while she was still alive. His evidence was that he pulled Billie-Jo towards him to assess the extent of her injuries, called 999 and then returned to the body. Forensic examiners found 158 bloodspots on his clothing, 76 spots on the trousers, 48 spots on the chest of his fleece jacket, 21 on the left sleeve and three on the right sleeve. There were 10 more on his left shoe. Almost all were invisible to the naked eye. DNA matching confirmed that this was all Billie-Jo's blood. A neighbour called to the scene confirmed that 'her head was completely shattered. You could see her brain and you could see her skull' (Mail Online, 2005). The neighbour also confirmed that Billie-Jo's head was lying on a bin liner, part of which was lodged inside her left nostril. When this was removed, there was a slow trickle of blood. The main forensic evidence against Jenkins at his trial were the blood droplets, which a forensic scientist 'successfully' argued were created as Jenkins swung the 18-inch tent peg, striking his foster-daughter at least nine times.

However, the defence contested this, arguing that the blood evidence supported his claim of finding Billie-Jo injured but not dead. Jenkins's conviction was eventually quashed in 2004 following a CCRC referral. The basis of the quashed conviction at the Court of Appeal was the concessions by the Crown's pathologist that evidence given at the first tribunal was inaccurate.

The Jenkins case illustrates the challenge for juries in deciding between which expert is 'correct' in their interpretation of the evidence. Jenkins was eventually acquitted by a majority verdict.

Undue weight given to DNA or forensic evidence also results in miscarriages of justice.[8] DNA has become the 'gold standard' by which a person can be placed at the scene of a crime, and recent advances in DNA mean that it can now produce results and evidence that would have been impossible even a decade ago. However, the statistics attached to DNA evidence by analysts can vary, and, in some cases, the statistical weight assigned to that match can vary enormously. The numbers provided to juries often overstate the evidence, and can result in a wrongful conviction (Gill, 2014). In addition to statistics, the way in which the evidence is collected, stored and analysed can also result in a wrongful conviction due to contamination (Gill, 2014, 2016). Juries risk being confused by the alleged certainty of DNA evidence (Findlay, 2008; Picinali, 2015), and the manner in which it is presented in cases has arguably led to some high-profile miscarriages. Juries may also be confused about the correct interpretation of the law in respect of a defendant's culpability. Indeed, issues relating to interpretation and changes in interpretation can cause miscarriages, as the next section illustrates.

Inappropriate use of the law

Zellick (2010: 14) identifies that another potential category of miscarriage of justice is where changes in case law (which advantage the defendant) may mean that a conviction is now unsafe. The law of joint enterprise provides a recent example of how a change in the interpretation of the law arguably renders an entire class of convictions unsafe. The House of Commons Justice Select Committee commented as follows:

> Has use of the doctrine of joint enterprise led to miscarriages of justice? The usual definition of a miscarriage of justice is a case in which somebody is convicted for a crime which they did not commit. The low rate of success of appeals against joint enterprise convictions is seen by some, including the DPP [Director of Public Prosecutions], as giving comfort that miscarriages of justice in this sense are not taking place to a significant degree. However, we have already noted ... that there are particular difficulties with bringing successful appeals in joint enterprise cases. Furthermore, concerns about the impact of the joint enterprise doctrine are not primarily focused on whether it is being misapplied in individual cases. The concerns are, rather, with whether

the doctrine, as it has developed through case law and is now being applied, is leading to injustices in the wider sense, including through a mismatch between culpability and penalty. (Parliament, 2014)

In *R v Jogee* [2016] UKSC 8, the Supreme Court examined the mental element of intent, which must be proved when a defendant is accused of being a secondary party to a crime (joint enterprise). The question of law for the court to consider was whether the common law took a wrong turning in two cases, *Chan Wing-Siu v The Queen* [1985] 1 AC 168 and *Regina v Powell and English* [1999] 1 AC 1. In considering the question of secondary liability, the Court's consideration was the person who did not themselves forge the document, fire the gun or stab the victim (the person who did is called 'the principal'), but who is said to have encouraged or assisted the principal to do so. The basic detail of *Chan Wing-Siu* and *Powell and English* was that where a defendant (D1), in committing a crime (crime A), then commits a second crime (crime B), the mental element required of the secondary party (D2) is simply that he foresaw the possibility that D1 might commit crime B. If D2 did foresee this, the cases treated his continued participation in crime A not simply as evidence that he intended to assist crime B, but as automatic *authorisation* of it. So, D2 was guilty under this rule even if he did not intend to assist crime B at all. This set a lower test for D2 than for D1, who will be guilty of crime B only if he has the necessary mental element for that crime, usually intent. However, the Supreme Court concluded that the correct rule on secondary liability is that foresight is simply evidence (albeit sometimes strong evidence) of intent to assist or encourage, which is the proper mental element for establishing secondary liability.

The Supreme Court's decision effectively reinforced the original doctrine on joint enterprise by reversing an interpretation of the law that had held sway for some time, so that mere bystanders may not be guilty of crimes. The Court explained that intention to assist is not the same as desiring the outcome of the principal's action, so a secondary party may be guilty of a crime to which they were opposed. The Court further clarified that the intention to assist may sometimes be conditional, in the sense that the secondary party hopes that the further crime will not be necessary, but if he nevertheless gives his intentional assistance on the basis that it may be committed if the necessity for it arises, he will be guilty. Accordingly, the Court considered that it would be a question for the jury *in every case* to determine whether the intention to assist or encourage is shown to be consistent with contemporary provisions in the Serious Crime Act 2007 of intentionally encouraging or assisting the commission of a crime. The Supreme Court clarified that a person is not to be taken to have had that intention merely because of foreseeability.

Commentators suggested that the inappropriate use of the law of joint enterprise opened up the possibility that there would be a plethora of appeals on the grounds that the misapplication of the law had caused a miscarriage of justice (Bowcott, 2016; Hopkins, 2016; McCarthy, 2016). There could well be future cases where gang members who are bystanders rather than principal actors will no longer be convicted of murder under long-standing principles of joint enterprise; however, at time of writing, it appears that the change in the law will not lead to mass prison releases (Rozenberg, 2016).[9]

Conclusion

This chapter has explored causes of miscarriages of justice, with a preliminary examination of how cognitive bias impacts on investigative processes and a discussion of the role of inadequate counsel and problems caused where evidentiary rules (such as disclosure of evidence) are somehow not followed. Chapter Four deals with investigative practices in detail and also assesses CJS reforms intended to reduce the negative impacts of poor investigative practice and the extent to which these can cause miscarriages. However, this chapter has identified investigative problems, particularly false confession, disclosure problems and other evidentiary issues, as causes of miscarriages because of the effect that they can have on later proceedings that result in a wrongful conviction. As Leo and Ofshe (1998: 429) put it, in a CJS 'whose formal rules are designed to minimize the frequency of unwarranted arrest, unjustified prosecution, and wrongful conviction, police-induced false confessions rank amongst the most fateful of all official errors'. As confessions are treated as damning, compelling and conclusive evidence of guilt, it becomes difficult for defence solicitors to undo the harm caused by a confession, even where this may later be recanted. On the whole, false confessions are arguably less of a problem in the UK today than they are in the US, where a different interrogational approach exists (Walsh et al, 2016). However, cuts in legal aid that may impact on the quality of defence representation afforded to a defendant, particularly in respect of flawed or lack of scrutiny of unused material or lacking resources to examine non-disclosure issues in depth, run the risk of compounding the problems that a defendant faces at trial. Concerns have also been raised that the fixed-fee legal aid system now leads to suspects' solicitors persuading clients to plead guilty, with the suggestion that some may be pleading guilty to crimes that they did not commit (Baksi, 2014; McConville and Marsh, 2014; Dugan, 2015). Criminal trials represent the might of the state against a defendant with considerably fewer resources, and so the best expedient defence (Merchant, 2011) may not be enough to combat the case brought by the state. Added to this, the ability of the prosecution to draw extensively on expert and scientific evidence that juries may well treat as *fact* rather than as a *possible* indicator of guilt arguably stacks the deck against the 'average' defendant.

Questions for further consideration

1. What are the primary causes of miscarriages of justice? Give reasons for your answer.

2. What is 'The Prosecutor's Fallacy'? Why is it important in discussing miscarriages of justice?

3. What difficulties exist for juries in considering expert testimony?

Notes

[1] See, for example, *Khan v the United Kingdom* (Appl. No 35394/97), ECHR 2000-V, where the police had installed covert listening devices on private property without the knowledge or consent of the owner. However, in admitting the evidence, the domestic court had taken proper account of the issue of unfairness and (then) lack of regulation. Thus, while the claim of interference with the right to a private life was upheld, the ECtHR did not uphold the complaint concerning a breach of Article 6 and the right to a fair trial.

[2] Section 76(2) of PACE specifies that confessions obtained by oppression or in other circumstances that cause doubt about the reliability of the confession shall be excluded (unless the prosecution proves to the court beyond reasonable doubt that this was not the case). For the purposes of Section 76 of PACE, oppression includes torture, inhuman or degrading treatment, and the use or threat of violence (whether or not amounting to torture).

[3] It should be noted that police officers were put on trial in respect of the Cardiff Three case but the trial collapsed, in part, due to the loss of prosecution files that were later found (Peachey, 2013).

[4] See *Benham v UK* [1996] 22 EHRR 293 and *Granger v UK* [1990] 12 EHRR 469.

[5] See, for example, *Salduz v Turkey* 36391/02 [2008] ECHR 1542, at para [51].

[6] In respect of Adams' claim for compensation, see further discussion in Chapter Six.

7   It should be noted that provisions exist in PACE and under the Criminal Justice Act 2003 for evidence to be excluded at trial.

8   It should, however, be noted that the use of DNA evidence to re-examine historical cases is a significant factor in post-conviction acquittals.

9   We note that, at the time of writing, several appeals that sought to overturn joint enterprise convictions have failed.

FOUR

Criminal investigation and miscarriages of justice

Sam Poyser and Rebecca Milne

Introduction

> Criminal investigation and miscarriages of justice are ...
> joined at the hip. (Savage and Milne, 2007: 610)

Miscarriages of justice injure individuals and society (see Chapter Five); however, they can also have constructive consequences by providing lessons that we can learn from. As Chapter Two noted, England and Wales have, over the last century, seen reforms that have made positive impacts through, for example, altering the practice of criminal justice professionals. These reforms were connected to critical failures that occurred in specific cases. Some were also connected to the results of research conducted into the causes of miscarriages. This research has been invaluable in revealing that many of the lessons taught by miscarriages relate to the processes and procedures involved in criminal investigation (Poyser and Milne, 2015). Furthermore, researchers have advised upon, and aided the implementation of, improvements to those processes and procedures, with the aim of reducing the occurrence of miscarriages (Stelfox, 2007; Williams, 2015).

This chapter will consider the role of criminal investigation in causing miscarriages in England and Wales and how research has contributed to change agendas, which have, in turn, influenced legislative, policy and practice reforms. As the chapter progresses, it will become evident that not only do processes and procedures associated with criminal investigation contribute to miscarriages, but the lessons learnt from miscarriages and from research relating to them have also contributed enormously to the ways in which criminal investigations are conducted.

The chapter will begin by very briefly revisiting research that has revealed the causes of miscarriages (see Chapter Three), demonstrating, as it does, that many are linked to criminal investigation. The chapter will next highlight how research has aided our comprehension of the causes that are connected to criminal investigation. In doing so, it will spotlight issues surrounding: (1) the investigative *process* generally; and (2) interview *practices and procedures* specifically. Official responses to research findings and improvements made to these processes, practices and procedures as a result are also discussed. The chapter ends by highlighting the need for further research in this area.

Pinpointing the link between criminal investigation and miscarriages of justice

The first major research study to identify and examine the causes of miscarriages was published by Borchard in 1932. This study, together with subsequent research in the UK and the US, has revealed similar findings (see, eg, Frank and Frank, 1957; Radin, 1964; Brandon and Davies, 1973; Bedau and Radelet, 1987; Connors et al, 1996; Leo and Ofshe, 2001; Naughton, 2007; Huff and Killias, 2013), which are that despite there being a multiplicity of causes of miscarriages (see Chapter Three), those that occur most frequently are linked to criminal investigation (Cutler, 2012). They include: (1) unreliable confessions; (2) non-disclosure of evidence; (3) reliance on circumstantial evidence; (4) fabrication of evidence; and (5) unreliable cell confessions (Forst, 2013). Building upon such findings, the body of research that has made the biggest impact in terms of reducing the occurrence of these particular causes is that conducted by psychiatrists and psychologists (Gudjonsson, 2003). This research has helped to explain such phenomena and has suggested improvements to processes and procedures involved in criminal investigation. The following discussion outlines some key findings of this research and their subsequent impact on reducing some types of miscarriages.

The investigative process and miscarriages of justice

Many wrongful convictions have clearly exemplified the contribution of the investigative process to causing miscarriages, from cases such as that of George Edalji in the late 1800s (see Chapter Two) through to that of the Drax environmental protestors, whose convictions were quashed in 2014 due to 'a complete and total failure to disclose evidence gathered by [an] undercover police officer' (Lord Thomas, cited in Evans, 2014). However, the miscarriages that focused a spotlight on the police investigative process more strongly than ever before, and indeed ever since, are those associated with the 1970s' 'Irish cases' (exposed between 1989 and 1991) (May, 1994). For example, after the successful appeal of the Guildford Four in 1989, it was revealed that the police had abused these individuals and manipulated evidence to fit the case they wished to present at trial (Rose, 1996). At face value, the causes of these miscarriages included false confessions (see Chapter Two); however, we might ask *why* confessions became such a focus of the investigation in the first place (Poyser and Milne, 2015). A possible answer is that the problems that led to these and other miscarriages go deeper (Findley, 2012). In fact, they arguably go back to the primary stages of an investigation, when police officers *believed* that they had the 'right' person/people and set about seeking to confirm this belief (see Chapter Three). From this perspective, these miscarriages were by-products of cognitive phenomena that resulted in problematic investigative decision-making and ultimately incompetence and/or wrongdoing (Williamson et al, 2013; Findley and O'Brien, 2014).

Police investigations set out to find the answers to two overarching questions: 'What, if anything, happened?' and 'Who, if anyone, did it?' (Milne and Bull, 2016). Research in this area has helped us to understand how investigators make decisions and the factors that compromise the reliability of their decision-making (Ask and Granhag, 2005). It has identified that a phenomenon pivotal to many miscarriages is the 'premature closure' of investigations. Although this concept was first introduced in the context of police interviewing (see Shepherd and Milne, 1999: 26), it is applicable to the entire investigative process in that investigations that start with 'investigator openness' to consider several lines of inquiry close prematurely around a particular 'thesis' involving a particular suspect(s) (Poyser and Milne, 2015). From then on, working on the premise that they have the guilty person, factors such as tunnel vision, belief perseverance and confirmation bias coalesce towards 'successful' case construction, with officers 'selectively weav[ing] together … information … to produce a simplified … coherent story' (Sanders et al, 2010: 368). Premature closure, then, is linked to 'case construction' in that once a suspect is identified, the investigation changes from being an objective search for 'What happened?' and 'Who did it?', to being a search for information to construct a case that supports the theory that the suspect is the culprit (McConville et al, 1991; Maguire and Norris, 1993). This change has involved investigators focusing on a conclusion and filtering all information in a case through the narrow lens provided by it (see Chapter Three). Information validating the conclusion is elevated in significance and information inconsistent with it is deemed insignificant (Poyser and Milne, 2015). This tunnel vision is both the *result* of fixation on a certain suspect (bias) and the *reason* for a one-sided search for more incriminating evidence or an interpretation of evidence as incriminating (bias confirmation), even when facts point in a contrary direction (belief perseverance) (Ask et al, 2008). Quite simply, the investigator *unconsciously* assigns too much weight to evidence that reinforces their hypothesis and too little to that which does not, and adheres to a belief despite evidence discrediting it (Findley and O'Brien, 2014).

Cognitive biases may not only affect early evidence gathering; they may also have a domino effect, impacting upon decisions made by others involved in the criminal justice system (CJS), such as prosecutors and expert witnesses (Findley, 2012). This may explain how innocent individuals sometimes find themselves on trial with a seemingly solid case against them (Eady, 2003). Indeed, as a victim of a miscarriage, in research conducted by the first author of this chapter (see Chapters Five and Seven), stated:

> once you are charged with a high-profile murder, you get a
> snowball effect ... the CPS [Crown Prosecution Service] ...
> rubber stamp what the police say, [in] court you get found
> guilty.... It just rolls and rolls until it's too late.

Many miscarriages seem to highlight that investigators in specific cases may have operated on predetermined notions of guilt (Poyser and Milne, 2011). Often, these cases involve individuals 'known' to the police through previous convictions who have become the early focus of investigations, resulting in officers neglecting other investigative leads (Savage and Milne, 2007). Internal and external pressures placed upon investigators in particularly horrific murder cases may also cause them to focus upon *speed* in bringing the case to a conclusion as their primary aim and to an 'ends'- rather than 'means'-oriented investigation (Klockars, 1980). This may, in turn, create the conditions for wrongdoing. Feeling certain of a suspect's guilt, the closed mindset of investigating officers may tempt them to move beyond unintentionally constructing a case around a suspect, to intentionally suppressing and/or eradicating all information that *does not* fit, and/or constructing information to ensure that it *does* fit with the original 'guilt' narrative (Savage and Milne, 2007). Such factors have been found to be major causes of wrongful conviction (Scheck et al, 2000). They may also be responsible in some investigations that fail to bring anyone to justice, as failure to investigate a crime may be due to premature investigative closure involving 'case denial'. Here, the investigative mindset is closed to a particular theory, meaning that officers fail to gather evidence with this in mind (Savage et al, 2007).

Research findings have provided information on the role of cognitive weaknesses in investigative processes and have fed into recommendations for improving and professionalising the investigative process in the UK, thereby helping to reduce miscarriages. Indeed, it was a specific miscarriage – the failure to investigate the murder of Stephen Lawrence – that drove such recommendations through into policy and practice (Savage et al, 2007). MacPherson's (MacPherson of Cluny, 1999) inquiry into police failings that contributed to causing the Lawrence miscarriage pinpointed investigative lessons to be learnt (ACPO, 2012). These included the need to confront the cognitive biases that had dominated the investigation. One way in which MacPherson felt that such biases could be confronted was through robust review and oversight of the investigative process and decisions made throughout it, so that if mistakes/miscalculations are made early on, procedures may aid in rectifying them at a later stage. It was believed that greater openness in investigations would help confront the issue of premature case closure (Savage and Milne, 2007). MacPherson recommended that the Association of Chief Police Officers (ACPO) devise codes of practice to govern such reviews, a recommendation later reinforced in the inquiry into the investigative failures surrounding the death of Victoria Climbié (Laming, 2003).

In 2006, ACPO revised their policy on major crime investigation in the *Murder investigation manual* (MIM) so as to institutionalise formalised review of investigations (ACPO, 2006). The Professionalising Investigation Programme (PIP), launched in 2005, further aimed to enhance the investigative process via investigator training and assessment (Centrex, 2005a, 2005b). Additionally, the Core Investigative Doctrine (Centrex, 2005b) advised investigators against rushing to premature judgements regarding the meaning of material gathered and encouraged them to challenge gut instincts, possess a healthy scepticism, seek to disprove their theory and create alternative theories (Savage and Milne, 2007). However, putting such advice into practice is often difficult, as the recent police handling of *some* child abuse allegations demonstrates.

Failures to investigate in the post-Savile era

The difficulties experienced by victims of child sexual abuse, particularly those who only feel able to report it as an adult, are well documented and include being disbelieved or punished for reporting their victimisation (Newby, 2012). The dreadful impacts of these crimes are indisputable; however, this should have no influence upon the police investigative process into such allegations (Jenkins, 2015). In order to avoid all forms of miscarriages and ensure that justice is done for everyone involved in such cases, *process* matters (White, 2016). In relation to the investigation of allegations of historic child sexual offences, this process has received much criticism. Such investigations are layered with complications, particularly as they effectively amount to one person's word against another's concerning an alleged event that took place decades ago (Hewson, 2014).

Many years ago, just this problem led to the development in the UK of an investigative policing method known as 'trawling': 'the police practice of making unsolicited approaches to former residents from … institutions under investigation' (Home Affairs Select Committee, 2002: i). Trawling has been termed 'investigation in reverse' (Newby, 2016), involving a process whereby the need for evidence to support the allegation has almost completely vanished (Webster, 2009). Clearly, this method may generate false allegations and possibly lead to miscarriages of justice.

In the late 1990s/early 2000s, various historic sexual abuse allegations were made by former residents of children's homes and other institutions against former staff who had worked there (Walker and McCartney, 2008). The police investigations that ensued engaged 34 out of 43 police forces in England and Wales and involved officers visiting former residents and giving them the opportunity to allege abuse (Eady, 2003). Many allegations made were based on events claimed to have occurred two or three decades earlier. This seriously undermined the ability of those accused to raise a robust defence (Poyser, 2012). In fact, all that they could do was deny it. Concern regarding the safety of the resulting convictions in many of these cases culminated in a report by the Home Affairs Select Committee (2002), which stated that a new genre of miscarriages of justice had arisen from the overenthusiastic pursuit of such allegations. These miscarriages included that of Anver Sheikh, wrongly convicted of serious sexual offences against two residents of a North Yorkshire care home in 2002 (Woffinden, 2004). His was one of a number of convictions eventually quashed amid a climate that saw trawling discredited (Newby, 2012). These wrongful convictions demonstrated that simply relying on the *volume* of complainants making allegations is not enough, particularly when they have been approached by the police rather than the other way round. The very real dangers of memory contamination and mistaken memories, discussed later in this chapter, played out in these, and other, case examples, where some of the most dreadful claims of sexual abuse were simply not true (Newby, 2012). In response to the Home Affairs Select Committee's (2002) report, trawling as an investigative method fell out of favour – that is, until around a decade later, when the celebrity Jimmy Savile died.

Almost immediately after his burial in 2011, stories began to emerge that Savile had committed abhorrent sexual crimes against primarily young girls. Importantly, in a programme made before he died, Savile denied being a paedophile but added 'How does anyone know whether I am or not?' (cited in Moore, 2013). This sums up the central problem surrounding historic abuse investigations, namely, trying to ascertain what actually happened many years ago. As Operation Yewtree (an investigation into allegations of abuse by Savile) and other similar police operations have found, the 'truth' is extremely difficult to establish (Moore, 2013).

Since Savile's death, many allegations have been made about a succession of public figures, including celebrities, politicians and senior police officers, and an investigative process similar to trawling appears to be in operation again. However, rather than visiting individuals to ask if they have been the victim of sexual abuse, police have appeared on websites inviting the public to name any high-profile person they think may have sexually abused them in the past, adding that they will remain anonymous and may gain compensation (Jenkins, 2015). Those accused are at the mercy of a media that has revealed their names, a history that cannot be revisited and a 'no-smoke-without-fire' narrative involving allegations that are almost impossible to refute. Up until recently, they were also at the mercy of a 'no-doubt' policy advocated by Her Majesty's Inspectorate of Constabulary (HMIC), which, in 2014, ordered detectives to automatically believe people who allege such abuse (Dodd, 2016b). It added: 'The presumption that a victim should always be believed should be institutionalised' (cited in Newby, 2016) – a problematic statement as it assumes that because allegations were made, offences were committed (ie that *allegations* are *facts*) (Moore, 2013).

Criticism of Operation Midland, which investigated claims of historic child sexual abuse and murder committed by establishment figures in a VIP paedophile ring during the 1970s and 1980s, further highlighted problematic issues in this area. These individuals were never charged (as police investigations uncovered no evidence to support allegations), but they were named in the media (Dodd, 2016a). The damage to their reputations was done. In March 2016, Operation Midland was shut down and the then Metropolitan Police Commissioner Bernard Hogan-Howe announced that the policy of automatically believing complainants would be dropped, adding: 'a good investigator would go and test the accuracy of the allegations and the evidence with an open mind.... This is a more neutral way to begin, than saying we should believe victims' (cited in Dodd, 2016b).

Miscarriages such as that of Anver Sheikh have shown that some people *do* make false allegations and that multiple complaints do not necessarily mean that they are true (Newby, 2012). As the policy documents discussed earlier recommend, allegations must be tested through robust, fair and professional investigation that determines whether there is evidence to support/contradict them. This supports a possible victim and reduces the risk of a miscarriage of justice.

Criminal investigation is often unimaginably difficult and challenges remain in terms of ensuring that it is undertaken professionally (Milne, 2016). Some of the policy changes that have occurred in the last decade are, indeed, positive developments; however, we must not be complacent. Indeed, we may need to go further in order to encourage mindsets that ensure effective, fair investigation (Stelfox, 2011). Arguably, as part of their training, investigators should be encouraged to analyse specific miscarriages of justice in order to confront the learning opportunities they present and to acknowledge that they are a very real problem. As the recent case of Barri White and Keith Hyatt indicates, a selective investigation, based upon who investigators *thought* (erroneously as it turned out) were the guilty parties, resulted in their failure to follow up alternative lines of enquiry and two miscarriages of justice (Shorter, 2013). Clearly, cognitive biases continue to impede investigator decision-making, meaning that further research is critical. The same is true of the police interview process.

Investigative interviewing and miscarriages of justice

In 1980, Irving and Hilgendorf highlighted the dearth of research on the police custodial questioning process in England and Wales. Much has changed since this time, and thankfully so, as issues relating to this process have been found to be a major cause of miscarriages, particularly in terms of the link between poor questioning and false confessions (Gudjonsson, 2003).

From ancient times, agents of the state have attempted to obtain information from suspects about their involvement in alleged crimes, often using threats and/or physical violence (Roberts, 2012). Perhaps unsurprisingly, false confessions were common. One of the least disputed of these was that of John Perry for the murder of his master, William Harrison, in 1661. This is because the alleged murder victim turned up alive (claiming to have been abducted) two years after Perry's execution (Gudjonsson, 2003: 166). After intense questioning by the Justice of the Peace, Perry not only falsely confessed to Harrison's murder, but implicated his brother and mother, who were executed alongside him (Ayling, 1984). However, we must 'fast-forward' 300 years to the 1970s in order to find *the* case that provides the 'most blatant and obvious example' of the role of the police interview process in causing miscarriages (Price and Caplan, 1977: 122). As Chapter Two outlined, the injustices relating to the arrest, false confessions and convictions of Colin Lattimore, Ronnie Leighton and Ahmet Salih for the murder of Maxwell Confait in 1972 were overturned at the Court of Appeal in 1974. Here, it was highlighted that the boys' confessions had been obtained under pressure placed upon them by interviewing officers (Poyser and Milne, 2015).

The 1977 Fisher Inquiry into the case revealed numerous police failings relating to the boys' interviews. These included their failure to: (1) ensure that an independent adult was present in order to safeguard the rights of these vulnerable suspects during questioning; (2) allow the boys access to legal advice; and (3) make an independent record of the alleged confessions made during the lengthy interviews (McBarnet, 1978: 455–63). The problems associated with this case framed the focus of the Royal Commission on Criminal Procedure (RCCP, 1981). Having been tasked in 1978, with studying and making recommendations on the workings of pre-trial procedures in England and Wales, the nature and fairness of the custodial questioning process were the focus of the RCCP's concerns. It therefore instructed that reviews and research into this process be conducted, and 12 studies were subsequently produced, seven by psychologists and five by lawyers (Gudjonsson, 2003). The RCCP (1981) pinpointed how the interview process is unavoidably psychologically coercive and highlighted the effects of custody on suspects, particularly those with vulnerabilities. It also advocated the need for the interview process to yield reliable information (Steer, 1981). Psychological research into police working practices authorised by the RCCP additionally established that during questioning, police were placing priority on gaining a confession over trying to discover what had actually happened in criminal cases. This was leading some officers to take advantage of suspects' vulnerabilities and/or to question them in an overbearing manner (Baldwin and McConville, 1981; Irving, 1980; Irving and Hilgendorf, 1980; Softley, 1981). In this respect, Irving's (1980) study is particularly noteworthy because it not only observed the interviewer, but also the mental state of the interviewee. In terms of the latter, it found that many suspects showed signs of distress and seemed to be in an abnormal mental state *prior* to questioning. Causes of distress included: unfamiliarity with surroundings; isolation from social contact; and feeling totally controlled by the police. Around 50% of suspects were judged by Irving to be mentally disturbed in some way *during* questioning. Indeed, they were 'not in a normal mental state [due to] intoxication, mental handicap, personality problems ... other predisposed problems ... or the character of custodial interrogation itself' (Irving, 1980: 136). Irving had highlighted a crucial issue relating to the police custodial setting, namely, that many people, including those *without* predisposed problems, may be vulnerable in this situation. In terms of their questioning of suspects, Irving (1980) found that in about 75% of cases studied, police used persuasive/manipulative techniques, including influencing suspects' perception of the consequences of confession, to 'make it easier' for them to confess and advising them that it was in their best interests to do so. On the basis of these and other findings, changes to police interview methods were recommended.

Unfortunately, the use of threats and pressure by some officers during questioning continued post-RCCP (Smith, 1983: 325). Clearly, the Judges' Rules governing proper procedures for the custodial questioning of suspects (see Chapter Two) were inadequate, as the Commission had highlighted (Price and Caplan, 1977). However, the RCCP (1981) had set out a 'blueprint' for a fair, practicable and effectual system of custodial questioning, and this was soon to pave the way for radical change to the CJS (Eddleston, 2009). This arrived in the form of the Police and Criminal Evidence Act 1984 (PACE) and its Codes of Practice (Section 66), which provided a legislative underpinning for the operation of police powers, suspects' rights and the regulation of custodial questioning – changes aimed at securing *fairness* and *transparency* in the process (Sanders et al, 2010). PACE laid down new requirements covering the detention, treatment and questioning of suspects in custody, including the obligation to record interviews with suspects and inform them of their right to free legal advice. It also moved to ensure that vulnerable suspects were treated fairly (Poyser and Milne, 2015).[1]

The establishment's recognition of the causes of injustice so starkly highlighted in the Confait case may have helped drive through reform; however, unfortunately, police interviews remained poor and continued to prioritise gaining *a confession* over *a reliable account* of 'what happened' in relation to alleged crimes (McConville et al, 1991). Indeed, in cases involving the most serious crimes, some of the most persuasive tactics identified by Irving were still being used (Irving and McKenzie,

1989). Additionally, an analysis by Baldwin (1992, 1993) of 400 police interviews in England around this time found serious problems at various stages of the questioning process. These included police interviewers reading the caution in a casual, hurried, incorrect and/ or incomprehensible manner. In terms of the interview itself, Baldwin found general ineptitude, poor technique (including interruptions) and assumptions of guilt. Worryingly, Baldwin (1993: 333) stated that despite their link to the causes of miscarriages, 'persuasive interviewing techniques' were still apparent in some cases. Certainly, miscarriages involving false confessions continued to occur, as demonstrated by the exposure of injustices in, for example, the Cardiff Newsagent Three (O'Brien, 2009) and the Cardiff Three (Sekar, 2013) cases in 1987 and 1988, respectively. These and other miscarriages demonstrated that some individuals continued to endure poor police questioning, and measures to safeguard suspects were failing. The Cardiff Newsagent Three case had involved numerous abuses of PACE in terms of police treatment of the suspects, including off-the-record interviews (Sekar, 1998), and in the Cardiff Three case, as Chapter Three highlights, one suspect had endured 19 separate interviews, involving oppressive questioning, over four days (Walker and McCartney, 2008).

Such high-profile malpractice led to demands for urgent reform from influential corners of society. These were significantly strengthened by successful appeals in the 'Irish cases' around this time (see Chapter Two) and resulted in the establishment of the Royal Commission on Criminal Justice (RCCJ) in 1991. Its task was to examine the workings of the CJS from the stage at which an offence is reported to police, through to the stage when a defendant has been found guilty and exhausted their right to appeal (RCCJ, 1993). In order to learn more about these issues, the RCCJ received evidence from over 600 organisations and commissioned 22 pieces of research (Gudjonsson, 2003). The RCCJ's report drew upon the findings of these studies (see, eg, Irving and Dunninghan, 1993), which provided empirical data on the conduct, role and working practices of criminal justice practitioners. They included analyses of the: (1) provision of custodial legal advice to suspects (McConville and Hodgson, 1993); (2) right to silence (Leng, 1993); and (3) extent to which suspects exercise it (Zander and Henderson, 1993). Additionally, some studies continued to examine custodial questioning (Moston and Stephenson, 1993) and the issue of protection for vulnerable persons in this setting (Evans, 1993; Gudjonsson, 1993). In particular, the latter study exposed the type and extent of vulnerabilities exhibited by suspects detained for interviewing and established that many are of low intelligence, have a learning disability or suffer from a significant intellectual impairment and exceptionally high levels of anxiety and distress. Crucially, it revealed that many of these intellectual deficits were unidentifiable from a brief clinical interview, meaning that they were effectively *invisible* to police officers (Gudjonsson, 2003). Taking such findings into account, it was clear that significant reforms to police interviewing techniques and training were required (Moston and Engleberg, 1993) and that the focus of custodial questioning must be placed upon a search for information, rather than a confession. This was a move supported by the RCCJ, which recognised in its subsequent report that gaining a confession remained investigators' priority and that this was contributing to causing miscarriages (McConville and Bridges, 1994), as well as by senior police officers such as Williamson (1994: 17), who stated that the police service had 'a serious skills deficit in its ability to obtain evidence through questioning'. There was certainly pressure for the police to implement a new approach to interviewing.

This approach began to materialise in the form of Home Office Circular 22/1992, in which certain principles relating to interviewing were developed as a result of collaboration between lawyers, police officers and psychologists (Gudjonsson, 2003). This document was supplemented by Home Office Circular 7/1993, which introduced a national one-week training course for basic interviewing skills (Williamson, 1994). Two booklets entitled *The interviewer's rule book* and *A guide to interviewing* accompanied the training and were issued to all 127,000 police officers in England and Wales (CPTU, 1992a, 1992b; see also Bull, 1999). The theoretical model on which the contents of these booklets were based created nationally agreed guidelines on interviewing suspects *and* witnesses (which, if breached, might result in a judge being unwilling to admit the statements in question into evidence). This new ethical approach to interviewing was the 'PEACE' interviewing model.

Developed by psychologists Rebecca Milne and Ray Bull in 1999, PEACE is an acronym that stands for the following stages of an investigative interview: (1) Planning and Preparation; (2) Engage and Explain; (3) Account; (4) Closure; and (5) Evaluation. PEACE focused on the importance of information gathering (before *as well as* during the questioning process), non-coercive interviewing and the accurate recording of interviews. It consisted of the 'Conversation Management' approach for more resistant interviewees (Shepherd, 1993; Shepherd and Griffiths, 2013) and the 'Cognitive Interview' for more cooperative ones (Fisher and Geiselman, 1992; Milne and Bull, 1999).

A subsequent national evaluation found that training in the use of the model had significantly improved the quality of suspect interviews in terms of officers' interviewing *styles* (eg they used fewer leading questions) and their adherence to PACE requirements (such as the need to notify suspects of their right to legal advice) (Clarke and Milne, 2001). However, the evaluation also revealed that one tenth of the interviews may have breached PACE and that interviewers' listening skills remained poor. Later research concluded that the PEACE model encouraged ethical interviewing and a fuller, more reliable, account from suspects (Soukara et al, 2009; Walsh and Bull, 2010), but highlighted a need for refresher training as some officers, over time, resumed their previous interview styles (Griffiths and Milne, 2006; Wright and Powell, 2006).

Further research-driven training for police officers came with the creation of the five-tiered structure of interviewing skills (a developmental approach tailored towards their career stages), which, from 2007, was incorporated into the PIP (Clarke and Milne, 2001), and the establishment of other aspects of investigative interviewing relating to vulnerable witnesses and the supervision and monitoring of interviews (Clarke and Milne, 2016). To date, research examining whether the five-tiered approach works, particularly at the advanced level, has indicated that if the correct individuals are selected for training, significant skill advancement is noticeable; however, it also found that the effectiveness of training for complex skills diminished over time, thereby reiterating the need for refresher training (Griffiths et al, 2011).

The more recent developments in interview training, 'unparalleled to [those] seen anywhere else in the world' (Gudjonsson, 2003: 55), have certainly improved interviewing skills and also encouraged the open-minded search for accurate information in the broader investigative context (Milne, 2016). However, as recent miscarriages have indicated, poor interviewing practices remain in some quarters (see Moody, 2012), and although these developments have resulted in less manipulative interviewing and consequently far fewer false confessions, some officers are *still* motivated by the desire to gain a confession (Bearchell, 2010: 71).[2] In other words, some officers fail to put into practice what they have learnt. However, it is not only suspects who are interviewed by police. On a daily basis, police officers of all ranks conduct interviews in different contexts and situations with victims and witnesses.

Interviewing victims and witnesses

Victims and witnesses are deemed by police officers themselves to be critical to criminal investigations (Sanders, 1986). They provide vital information not only in first reporting a crime, but also in supplying 'investigative steers' (eg through imparting descriptions of what they saw and who they saw doing it), as well as in later testifying in court (Sanders et al, 2010). Clearly, without their vital input, the CJS would crumble. Thus, we might consider how interviews with these individuals might contribute to causing miscarriages of justice and the lessons to be learnt in this context.

From the 1970s onwards, research in the US by Loftus (1979) and in the UK by Clifford and Bull (1978), as well as subsequent analyses conducted in different settings, have demonstrated that witnesses' testimony is extremely fallible. This is due to inherent problems with human memory, relating to: (1) the perception and encoding of crime-related information; (2) the retention of that information; and (3) the retrieval of that information (Wilcock et al, 2008). Memory is fragile, malleable and suggestible to internal and external influences (Milne, 2016). Indeed, as Loftus (2013) argues, it is 'like a Wikipedia page: You can go in there and change it, but so can other people'. Other people can include other victims and witnesses involved in a criminal event and, of course, police officers who wish to gain information from those who experienced it. Erroneous victim and witness testimony is a major cause of miscarriages worldwide and there are very recent UK cases where it has played a significant role (see Innocent, no date). Clearly, the police must provide victims and witnesses with the best possible opportunity to impart reliable accounts of their experiences. The methods used to find out the answers to the critical investigative questions of 'What happened?' and 'Who did it?' determine the quality and quantity of the information gained (Milne and Bull, 2016). In other words, police officers (and others) can influence *what* and *how much* information victims and witnesses report.

A recent analysis of victims' experiences of the CJS revealed that many felt victimised not only by the crime that they had suffered, but also by the treatment that they subsequently received by criminal justice professionals (Bowcott, 2015), which indicated a lack of empathy and understanding (Syal, 2016). This was particularly felt by the most vulnerable (including older and disabled individuals), many of whom have a higher risk of being victimised. Indeed, recent research has revealed that these individuals receive an inadequate service from nearly 75% of UK police forces (McVeigh, 2015). Certainly, even the smallest failure in the treatment of these individuals by criminal justice professionals may have tragic consequences (Starmer, 2016). Therefore, criminal justice practitioners, particularly the police (because they are usually the first agency to come into contact with victims and witnesses when a crime occurs), must treat these individuals with respect. They must also conduct successful interviews with them so as to enable their voices to be heard (Milne, 2016). Conversely, poor interviews may lead to miscarriages of justice, which have negative impacts upon the victim/witness and the wrongly convicted (Poyser and Milne, 2015).

As previously mentioned, with some exceptions, victims and witnesses take part in different types of 'interview' soon after they experience a criminal event. Such interviews may include those that occur, for example, when a victim or witness calls the emergency services, when they are at the scene of crime, and, later, when they (may) take part in a full investigative interview (Milne and Bull, 2016). However, no matter at what stage of the justice process they are interviewed, research is relatively consistent in finding that their questioning is generally poor (see, eg, Clarke and Milne, 2001; Griffiths and Milne, 2006). This is because their interviews are often police- rather than victim/witness-led, include the frequent use of leading questions (which can alter human memory) and are more often statement-focused than focused on gathering accurate/reliable information (Shepherd and Milne, 2006). The handwritten method of recording interviews with adult victims/witnesses is also problematic as this depends upon the police officer's memory of what was said, often therefore resulting in inaccuracies (Rock, 2001) and little detail and clarity (Conway, 2008).

In terms of the victim/witness initial call to the emergency services, researchers have found, for example, that call handlers who 'interview' victims/witnesses reporting crimes drive the interview and generally ask rather 'quick-fired', leading and/or suggestive questions (Ambler and Milne, 2006; Leeney and Muller-Johnson, 2011). Considering the circumstances, this is understandable; however, research has revealed that where a free-recall instruction is given to a victim/witness in this context, much more information is elicited from them than when 'quick-fire' questions concerning, for example, 'What?' and 'Where?' are asked (Pescod et al, 2013).

In terms of interviews with victims/witnesses at the crime scene, research has revealed that front-line inexperienced police officers, who are normally first to interview victims/witnesses (at/near crime scenes), feel undertrained and ill-equipped to do this (Dando et al, 2008a). As with call-handler interviews, these 'initial account' interviews are often conducted quickly (as there may be an immediate opportunity, based on information provided, to catch/arrest the perpetrator) (Gabbert et al, 2016). Again, this means that quick-fire, leading questions and frequent interruptions of the victim/witness characterise these interviews – all of which may contaminate their memory (MacDonald et al, 2016). The development and use by researchers of instruments such as the Self-Administered Interview (consisting of instructions and questions that enable victims/witnesses to provide their own uninterrupted account of events) have demonstrated that much more accurate/detailed information can be elicited than through a simple free-recall request (see Gabbert et al, 2009). Additionally, asking a victim/witness to make sketches as they recall events has also been found to be significantly more effective in aiding memory retrieval than simply asking them to recall events (Dando et al, 2008b). Advances in technologies being used by officers at scenes of crime, such as body-worn video cameras, are already offering new opportunities to gain more good-quality accurate information, and ongoing research is focused on this (Milne and Bull, 2016).

In terms of interviews with victims/witnesses that may occur at a later stage in an investigation, which may focus upon attempting to gain answers to further questions, a full investigative interview may occur. This aims to 'gain a full and faithful account to help investigators [make] informed decisions within the ongoing enquiry and to serve as evidence in court' (Milne and Bull, 2016: 183). Research has found that these interviews are often poor in terms of being interviewer-driven and including many leading and closed questions (Clarke and Milne, 2001). However, psychologists have developed tools to aid the police in achieving a greater amount of accurate information from such interviews. In particular, the Cognitive Interview (CI) (Fisher and Geiselman, 1992) – which asks interviewees to: (1) report everything; (2) mentally reinstate context; (3) recall events in different orders; and (4) change perspective – and the Enhanced CI (Fisher et al, 2011) – which encourages interviewers to: (1) explain the aims of the interview; (2) build rapport with interviewees; (3) engage in witness-compatible questioning; (4) probe topics utilising mental imagery; and (5) use varied methods of retrieval – have been found to be significantly more effective in terms of enhancing memory for accurate information than non-CI interviews (Milne and Bull, 2016).

In the UK, such positive findings have resulted in the development of a national approach to interviewing witnesses (in the PEACE model and five-tiered approach previously discussed) adopted by the police service. These tools have, to some extent, improved the quality and quantity of information gained from adult victims and witnesses during questioning (Clarke and Milne, 2001). However, as previously mentioned, research has demonstrated that some early-career-stage officers still feel unconfident in using such tools (Clarke et al, forthcoming; Griffiths et al, forthcoming). This is one of the reasons why psychologists have urged that *all* victim/witness interviews should be electronically recorded. This would ensure that all information reported is secured and that memories are largely 'unstained' by external influences (Wilcock et al, 2008). However, the introduction of such tools does not ensure that officers will put into practice what they have learnt. Poor police questioning, in some contexts, continues to lead to unreliable witness testimony (see Morrison, 2013). Such failures may be even more damaging in the context of interviews with vulnerable victims/witnesses.

As previously mentioned, procedures have been introduced over the last 15 years or so relating to interviewing vulnerable victims/witnesses, such as those who have impaired mental functioning, the elderly and children (Milne and Bull, 2016). Practitioner guidance and training relating to interviewing such groups in the form of, for example, Achieving Best Evidence in Criminal Proceedings (ABE), has been helpful in acting as a tool for these individuals to provide accurate accounts about their experiences of an alleged crime and for police to 'maximise the evidential value of the account [provided] ... for criminal courts' (Children's Commissioner, 2015: 14). However, some problems have been experienced in driving certain aspects of the training into practice. For example, a report by the Children's Commissioner (2015) found that ABE interviews with children were inconsistent in terms of quality. Additionally, a joint Her Majesty's Inspectorate report examining ABE interviews in child sexual abuse cases found that there was insufficient consideration of children's needs, insufficient preparation before they were questioned and interviews focused too often on concepts that were difficult for them to comprehend (HMCPSI and HMIC, 2015). There was also what was deemed to be inappropriate questioning (including leading questions) and, overall, poor compliance with the guidelines on gathering evidence in this context. Worryingly, the report concluded that the 'gap between best practice and actual practice is widening' and that training and guidance must be improved (cited in Bowcott, 2014).

Although the contribution of research to introducing evidence-based approaches/techniques into police training in order to improve victim/witness interviewing cannot be denied, it is even more important to ensure that *best* practice becomes *actual* practice. Victims and witnesses, whether considered vulnerable or not, must be given the best opportunity to provide accurate, reliable information regarding crime/s experienced so as to achieve justice for all (Gabbert et al, 2016).

Conclusion

Miscarriages of justice are inevitable in the CJS as they are generated by a multitude of factors that we will never be able to entirely eradicate (Eady, 2016). Nevertheless, we should arguably do all that we can in order to learn from these system failures and to minimise their future occurrence. As many of the causes of miscarriages relate to processes and procedures involved in criminal investigation, our effort should be particularly concentrated here. Research-driven changes to policy and practice have helped to tackle some of the causes of miscarriages in this area. In particular, research has aided us in understanding that: (1) good-quality, skilful investigation and interviewing of suspects will reduce reliance on gaining a confession and instead encourage a search for the truth; (2) careful but thorough interviewing of victims and witnesses will give them the opportunity to present their best evidence; and (3) a fuller understanding and awareness of vulnerable individuals when interviewing them will enable them to have a voice. Just as important, however, is the need for those working within the CJS to adhere to due process rules and regulations as they sometimes do not. Police officers, for example, sometimes still fail to comply with the regulations governing how they must obtain evidence, with disastrous results. By way of illustration, in 2012, a failure by a detective to follow the rules of PACE governing the way in which he interviewed killer Christopher Halliwell resulted in all of the evidence relating to Halliwell's confession and the discovery of one of two bodies being ruled inadmissible at trial and to Halliwell, initially at least, avoiding punishment for some of his crimes (Evans, M., 2012). Certainly, 'Where a detailed regime … is laid down in a statutory code … it is not for the police to substitute their own rules and procedures' (Naughton, 2013: 90). Undoubtedly, many lessons remain to be learnt in our attempts to reduce miscarriages of justice relating to criminal investigation.

Questions for further consideration

1. Savage and Milne (2007) argue that criminal investigation and miscarriages of justice are 'joined at the hip'. How far do you agree with this statement?

2. The last 50 years have seen major reforms occur in England and Wales that have positively impacted upon miscarriages of justice, for example, through altering the practice of criminal justice professionals. Why do you think these reforms occurred?

3. Many countries have not responded to the exposure of high-profile miscarriages in the way that England and Wales has, that is, they have not seen root-and-branch changes to policy, practice and legislation. Why do you think this might be?

Notes

[1] Another outgrowth of recommendations from the RCCP was the establishment of the CPS under the Prosecution of Offences Act 1985. This took over the prosecution function from the police.

[2] For further discussion on this and related issues, see also Quirk (2017).

FIVE

The victims of miscarriages of justice

Sam Poyser

Introduction

That utter feeling of helplessness … the system has taken over … a burning feeling of injustice. (Victim of a miscarriage of justice)

This statement, taken from the author's own empirical research, provides some insight into the experience of a victim of a miscarriage of justice and highlights, in particular, the sense of powerlessness and injustice felt by almost everyone who suffers a wrongful conviction. Miscarriages of justice cause wide-ranging and enduring harm, leaving victims with the 'ashes' of what they once had. Despite these often irreversible impacts, victims typically receive little support from the state upon release from prison (Tan, 2010). Virtually every victim of a miscarriage, or *exoneree*, loses respect for the criminal justice system (CJS), in part, because *their* offender – the state and its representatives – are rarely punished (Poyser, 2012), and this feeling can percolate outwards through indirect victims, such as relatives and communities (Jenkins, 2013a; 2013b). In addition, victims of the crimes at the centre of the miscarriage of justice become doubly victimised – first, by the crime itself and, second, by the exposure of the miscarriage – which returns them to the limbotic state of 'not knowing' experienced immediately after the crime occurred (Poyser, 2012). Miscarriages of justice are hugely damaging to society and costly in terms of the financial burden of imprisoning the wrong people (Naughton, 2001). Put simply, they devastate lives, undermine citizens' support for the CJS and damage wider society, their effects often still being felt decades after their exposure (Yant, 1991).

This chapter will begin by clearly delineating victims of miscarriages of justice *as* victims and considering who or what has offended against them. The findings of research on the harms of miscarriages will then be addressed, alongside discussion of the official response to these harms. The analysis will conclude by suggesting that much more needs to be done: first, by researchers to assess the harms associated with miscarriages; and, second, by the state and its criminal justice practitioners to address and minimise these harms. Importantly, where possible, the chapter will draw upon findings from empirical research conducted by the author of this chapter (discussed further in Chapter Seven). This research involved semi-structured interviews with a sample of individuals ($N = 39$) associated with miscarriage campaigns in England and Wales, including victims of wrongful conviction, members of their families, associates of their campaigns (including representatives from campaigning organisations, lawyers and expert witnesses) and other individuals comprising journalists, a police officer, a politician and a judge. Although the research set out to identify the key factors that lead to successful campaigns against miscarriages, in its execution, another dimension for analysis emerged, namely, the impact of specific miscarriages upon various victims. Before discussing the victims of miscarriages of justice, however, it is crucial to identify them *as* victims.

Victims of miscarriages of justice really are victims

A victim of crime can be defined as an individual who is 'harmed, injured or killed as a result of a crime, accident or other event or action' (Oxford English Dictionary, no date). However, as criminologist Richard Quinney (1972: 314) contends, the notion of 'victim' cannot be taken for granted. We feel that we instinctively know who, or what, is the victim in any given situation, simultaneously excluding others from this label. In other words, in reality, our conceptions of victims (and, indeed, of offenders) are optional and discretionary, meaning that 'the victim' is a social construction. From this critical-criminological perspective, and drawing from definitions of state crime provided by scholars such as Chambliss (1989) and Frederichs (2004), we may argue that victims of miscarriages of justice are victims of harms inflicted upon them by the state and its officials (as wrongful convictions occur in a CJS run by the state) in pursuit of their job. Indeed, Stratton (2014) places wrongful convictions firmly on a sliding scale of state crimes, moving from 'crimes of omission' (negligence/an absence of state involvement where it should have been present) to 'crimes of commission' (active or conscious state involvement/intentional rule- or law-breaking). In placing wrongful convictions alongside other state crimes, Stratton clearly identifies the state as the offender and those harmed by wrongful conviction as victims and claims that the state unconditionally holds power in these circumstances and should therefore be held accountable (Doyle, 2013). As we will see shortly, many victims of wrongful conviction suffer similar impacts to victims of state crimes, including, in some cases, forms of torture (Westervelt and Cook, 2010), with the offender, in the most part, avoiding accountability and punishment (Kauzlarich et al, 2001). Clearly, exonerees are fundamentally victims of the CJS and therefore 'victims of the State. They have been wrongly convicted ... as a result of explicit illegal state action or the misapplication of state power' (Westervelt and Cook, 2010: 261).

The identification of those who are harmed through wrongful conviction *as* victims is important because it distinguishes those who have suffered and affords them some dignity (Moffett, 2014: 21). Conversely, those who are not recognised as victims may suffer emotional injury and self-reproach. Delineation of the wrongly convicted as victims also allows us to compare their experiences with other victims. Contemporary discourses surrounding victimisation highlight the issue of secondary victimisation (Sellin and Wolfgang, 1964), whereby an individual is first victimised by virtue of a crime being committed but then goes on to feel re-victimised as a result of engaging with the CJS, through, for example, insensitive police questioning (Savage et al, 2007). Arguably, victims of miscarriages of justice are victimised in a similar manner. They are first victimised by being wrongly convicted and are then re-victimised by, for example, the appellate system's unwillingness to quash their conviction, the prison system's disallowance of their progression through to release (as will be discussed shortly) and, if their conviction is quashed, inadequate systems in place to help them to readjust to life after exoneration (Robins, 2015b).

In parallel with victims of crime, victims of wrongful conviction suffer a range of impacts as a result of their victimisation. Additionally, as with other victims, the impact of societal structures such as gender, race, age and class can be observed in victims of miscarriages, who are disproportionately young men from working-class backgrounds, unemployed or in casual/low-skilled jobs (Brandon and Davies, 1973; Naughton, 2007), and, in relation to particular types of wrongful conviction, such as those associated with the joint enterprise law, from minority ethnic communities (Egbuono, 2015). Just as some victims of crime feel a stigma associated with the particular form of victimisation that they have suffered, victims of miscarriages often find themselves stigmatised by a 'no-smoke-without-fire' narrative, fuelled by the fact that quashed convictions are not accompanied by an official declaration of innocence (Lean, 2007). Perversely, this situation also exists for those who are investigated in relation to particular offences and who are never ultimately charged. Indeed, as Sister Frances Dominica, recently barred from the children's hospice that she founded after sexual abuse allegations, for which she was investigated but never charged, stated: 'If you don't go to trial, you're never found innocent ... [you] are neither convicted of [offences] by a jury nor able fully to clear [your] name' (cited in Addley, 2016). After suffering such allegations, such individuals, who have included carers and teachers, as well as members of the clergy, find themselves in a permanent state of 'reputational limbo', excluded from their jobs because of safeguarding concerns yet unable to ever prove their innocence (Addley, 2016). Just like many victims of crime, victims of miscarriages seek answers to questions such as 'Why?' and 'How did this happen?' and often engage in campaigning activities aimed at trying to prevent such victimisation from occurring again, as a campaigner outlined to the author: "*some of them describe it as soldiers coming back from the First World War having left their colleagues behind and are just consumed with the injustice of what has happened to [others] ... they are campaigning because of that*".

As previously mentioned, the victims of miscarriages extend beyond the individual who has been wrongly convicted. They include the family of the exoneree and of the victim of the original crime (if deceased), communities from which the injured individuals come, the CJS, and society more generally. The impacts of miscarriages upon these victims are discussed in the following, beginning with the wrongly convicted themselves.

The impacts of miscarriages of justice upon the wrongly convicted

The accounts of exonerees, outlined in autobiographical or biographical texts (see, eg, Callan, 1998; Batt, 2004) and newspaper and TV interviews, furnish readers and audiences with detailed descriptions of the impact of their experiences. However, in terms of academic research, this issue has tended to be neglected in favour of studying the causes and scale of, as well as how to respond to and reduce, miscarriages. While research on the impact of miscarriages amounts to just a handful of studies, these analyses have revealed that exonerees experience multiple harms and that, in line with the findings of victimological research more broadly (Townsend and Asthana, 2009), such harms are experienced differently and to different degrees by each victim. Importantly, the following discussion primarily focuses upon impacts suffered by exonerees from the point of their release from prison as this is where the bulk of research findings lie. However, in reality, the impact of a miscarriage begins from the moment an individual first comes into contact with the CJS in connection with an offence (Chinn and Ratliff, 2009).

When a wrongly convicted individual is released from prison, images in the media are usually of the person celebrating their freedom alongside their supporters. The nightmare appears to us, as onlookers, to be over. For most, however, it has only just begun, as this exoneree in the author's research outlined:

> Your problems start when you walk out of prison ... I find it all difficult. Its just a bigger cage out here ... that's the way I look at it. Prison is a smaller cage. Trying to rebuild your life is the hardest part.

While in prison, victims have lost the 'guy ropes' that tied them to society. Indeed, as another commented: "*I lost my family, my home, my job ... absolutely everything*". Such impacts are often compounded for many victims because they have spent so long in prison. Within the prison system, those who are unwilling to confront 'their offending' are considered to be *in denial* of their offence (Naughton, 2005). The ability to show remorse influences many decisions made throughout the justice process. Refusal by the wrongly convicted to admit to offences and demonstrate remorse results in penal decisions to exclude such individuals from the normal routes of making progress through the system to parole (Clow et al, 2012). Therefore, they frequently serve sentences well past their original tariff (Tan, 2010) and, as a journalist who had exposed a long-running miscarriage outlined, suffer in all kinds of ways as a result: "*This thing about denial of guilt meant that these prisoners were badly treated ... there was pressure on them all the time to admit it*". When they are eventually released, exonerees report suffering psychological, behavioural, emotional and financial harms.

Psychological harms

The bulk of research on the impact of miscarriages of justice has focused upon the psychological harms experienced by exonerees. As a whole, this demonstrates that the individual emerges from prison profoundly changed and suffering severe and lasting psychological consequences (Campbell and Denov, 2004; Clow et al, 2012). Some of the most dramatic findings in this area are provided by Grounds (2004) and

Jamieson and Grounds (2005), who performed a number of psychiatric assessments of 18 exonerees in the UK. Their tests revealed that 14 out of 18 victims had permanent and irreversible personality change as a result of their experiences. This manifested itself in symptoms such as a chronic feeling of threat, estrangement, emptiness, irritability and loneliness. The researchers also found that 12 out of 18 victims had severe Post-Traumatic Stress Disorder (PTSD), of a form similar to that found in political prisoners (Grounds, 2004). Symptoms included flashbacks, withdrawal from communication, insomnia and paranoia. It was concluded that these problems were directly attributable to the individuals' wrongful arrests, convictions and imprisonment as none of them had experienced any psychiatric issues prior to conviction (Jamieson and Grounds, 2005: 25). This is further supported by the exonerees' families, many of whom described them as 'unrecognisable from how they used to be' (Grounds, 2004: 23). Importantly, Turnbull (2011), a leading expert on PTSD, suggests that the trauma experienced by the wrongly convicted is worse than that experienced by prisoners of war or hostages because victims of miscarriages have been detained by legal means within their *own* countries rather than by alien cultures.

Other research has likened the psychological trauma suffered by exonerees to that suffered by asylees and refugees, particularly in terms of the impact of sudden uprooting and displacement, which occurs at least twice for the wrongly convicted – first, when they are uprooted from society and, second, when they are uprooted from prison – both times without warning (Chinn and Ratliff, 2009). This research also suggests that experiences common to asylees, refugees and exonerees include: detention, torture, violence, separation from and loss of relatives, hardships, and exile. Research that studied 18 exonerees from death row in the US concluded that they had been psychologically traumatised in a way similar to victims of natural disasters, particularly in terms of the impact of being ripped from their families/communities (Westervelt and Cook, 2010). Other commentators have likened victims' experiences to those who have been kidnapped: 'Their experience will leave them with all the scars of a kidnap victim, but little of the recognition' (Bolton, 2015). Lastly, in a comment bolstering other research findings, an exoneree in the author's research commented: "*Being taken away from your family for something you haven't done is … inhumane*".

Crucially, the psychological impact of wrongful conviction outlined earlier is not generally found in prison effects research more widely. Indeed, aside from the 'pains of imprisonment' and forms of adaptation to prison culture described by Sykes (1958) and Clemmer (1958), psychological research shows little evidence of personality deterioration and psychiatric morbidity due to long-term incarceration (see, eg, Sapsford, 1978; Rasch, 1981). This dichotomy between the wrongly and rightly convicted is perhaps because the former's experience of the legitimacy of their incarceration is different (Grounds, 2004). The circumstances that the wrongly convicted individual has found themselves in are impossible to reconcile.

Behavioural harms

Exonerees' experience of a successful appeal and sudden release from prison can be conceptualised as a 'critical situation' (Giddens, 1984: 24) in which the accustomed behaviours and, indeed, routines of years of prison life become, within the space of a few hours and, crucially, with little or no warning, irrelevant (Tan, 2010). Many victims of miscarriages find it almost impossible to adapt to the realities of life on 'the outside' after such a routinised life on 'the inside' (Jenkins, 2014). Those who have spent many years in prison find fitting back into a society that has changed so much a challenge (Hill, 2010). Many experience a state of 'normlessness' (Durkheim, 1897), finding it incredibly difficult to reconnect with the changed society that they now find themselves in. As an exoneree in the author's research described: "*I came out and had no real sense of who I was or what I was doing*". Such problems may be exacerbated by a phenomenon called 'lost time', whereby exonerees may think of themselves as the age that they were when convicted (Grounds, 2004). This can create difficulties when trying to mix with peers on release, all of whom have progressed to different life stages.

Another behavioural change that research suggests may occur in some victims when released from prison is the adoption of avoidance behaviour (Jenkins, 2013a). Exonerees report taking definitive steps to avoid meeting new people due to finding it difficult to trust strangers. Campbell and Denov's (2004) research found that exonerees avoided authority figures, such as the police, for this reason. Many victims also demonstrate a preoccupation with always making sure that someone knows where they are (Westervelt and Cook, 2013).

In an attempt to cope with some of the issues mentioned, research suggests that some victims may engage in self-destruction, using drugs and alcohol in an attempt to disassociate from the problems they confront on a daily basis (Naughton, 2007). This, in turn, can lead to more intense physical health problems, as discussed shortly.

Emotional harms

Campbell and Denov's (2004) research found that when released from prison, the wrongly convicted often experience ongoing and profound emotional disorders and are prone to mood swings, emotional outbursts and despair. The author's research highlighted the 'emotional emptiness' felt by exonerees as a result of their experience. Similarly, research by Jenkins (2013a) revealed that exonerees found emotional intimacy with family members very difficult. Furthermore, Turner and Rennell's (1995) research found that the emotional gap between exonerated fathers and their children was similar to that which existed between children and their fathers who returned from the Second World War. Research suggests that where individuals have been wrongly convicted of murdering a member of their *own* family, different emotional harms may arise. For example, parents wrongly convicted of murdering their children, such as the solicitor Sally Clark, have the opportunity to grieve for their children stolen from them (Jenkins, 2014). They may also have other children taken into care resulting in emotional ties being damaged (Cannings, 2006).

Many exonerees report that feelings of anger and bitterness dominate their lives (Jenkins, 2013a). The author's own research highlighted that this anger may relate to the injustice not only that they have personally suffered, but also suffered by the family of (in this case) the murder victim: "*I [also] feel aggrieved for the victim's family [who, like me] ... have had no justice*". Research suggests that some of this anger is also associated with feelings of being stigmatised by the community to which one returns. Goffman (1963: i) described stigma as 'spoiled identity'. In other words, one's identity in society is tainted by a discrediting attribute. An issue that exonerees report feeling emotionally aggrieved about is that while they may have been exonerated in the courts, this is not the case in the eyes of the community (Naughton, 2007). 'Whispering campaigns' often surround them, as an interviewee in the author's research described: "*That stigma still lives ... some people still believe I did the crime*". This is partly because when the Court of Appeal quashes a conviction, it does not declare an individual innocent (Naughton and Tan, 2010). This situation may be compounded by the release of a police statement that they will not be reopening the investigation into the case (Cole, 2009), as a victim in the author's research outlined: "*the police say ... we are not looking for anyone else ... that feeds back to the public you know ... 'Ah well, the police must have known something we don't'*". Another felt that one is guilty in the eyes of the community until one can prove oneself innocent and that the media were responsible for this: "*Immediately after my conviction, most papers printed 'Monster' … that stigma, generated by the media, lasts after a conviction is quashed*".

Research suggests that stigma surrounding exonerees may be reduced if they received a public apology from the state (Westervelt and Cook, 2013), as one victim in the author's research argued: "*you need the public to recognise that something wasn't right … this comes with an apology*". This is supported by research in the US and UK which suggests that an official apology is not only a recognition of the harms inflicted upon an exoneree; it may act as a symbolic reinstatement of innocence, thereby restoring their reputation and aiding their reacceptance back into their community. Ultimately, this may help them to begin to emotionally heal (Tan, 2010). However, an apology is a luxury afforded to very few exonerees (Poyser, 2016).

Physical harms

Very little research has been conducted on the physical harms of wrongful conviction. This is despite the fact that anecdotal sources such as biographies and media reports indicate that, for some, they can be severe (see Batt, 2004). As previously mentioned, in order to cope with the challenges presented by their release from prison, some victims abuse their bodies through the use of drink and drugs, as this victim of a miscarriage outlined: "*Then my body went 'bang'. I ended up in hospital. I realised I had a problem…. So I went to see psychologists to help me … to get me off the drugs*". In some cases, such activities have resulted in the premature death of exonerees (see Shaikh, 2007). Others have died from conditions that may have been stress-related shortly after their release (McSmith, 2007). Additional physical impacts include the scars that have resulted from some exonerees' treatment by the authorities upon arrest/detention. Keith Twitchell and the Birmingham Six, for example, state that they were physically tortured into signing confessions by the notorious West Midlands Serious Crime Squad (Naughton, 2007). Many exonerees report having suffered physical violence committed by members of their community and local police officers after their release due to doubts concerning their innocence (see Maguire, 2008; O'Brien, 2009).

Financial harms

Despite many wrongly convicted individuals having a secure job and home life prior to being imprisoned, research demonstrates that wrongful conviction often robs them of these assets, meaning that when they leave prison, they are in immediate financial difficulty (Jenkins, 2013a). Exonerees receive little/no financial support with which to rebuild their lives (Tan, 2010). Most leave prison with a few hours' notice and a few pounds to cover their immediate costs as they depart the prison gates (Taylor and Wood, 1999). For example, after spending nearly 17 years in prison for a brutal rape he did not commit, Victor Nealon was released with three hours' notice, a train ticket and £46.00 (Robins, 2015a). Victims often have no close family to return to (due to familial break-ups while in prison) and find themselves using night shelters or sleeping rough (Jenkins, 2013a).

The public perception may be that it is normal for victims to receive large sums of compensation relating to their wrongful conviction. In reality, over 99% of successful appellants are ineligible for payment (Naughton, 2013: 212). This situation worsened when the ex-gratia compensation scheme was abolished in favour of a more restrictive approach to awarding compensation (Naughton, 2013). Amendments to the statutory compensation scheme for victims of miscarriages made under the Criminal Justice and Immigration Act 2008 (see Chapter Six) not only capped the amount of compensation that may be awarded at a lower level than previously, but served to restrict compensation to those who can demonstrate their innocence 'beyond reasonable doubt' – most perplexing considering that this is not required in order for the CJS to grant a successful appeal (Taylor and Wood, 1999). Such changes now 'make an award of compensation almost impossible to achieve' (Robins, 2015b).

Importantly, where compensation *is* awarded, a government assessor may deduct the costs of 'bed and board' – costs the appellant would have been required to pay out of their income for mortgage/rent and food had they not been wrongly imprisoned (Naughton, 2013). As an exoneree stated in 2009, the decision to take £37,158 out of his award of £650,000 for what were termed 'saved living expenses' (see also Chapter Six) was 'the final insult' (O'Brien, 2009: 198). Interestingly, the author's research highlighted an additional problem experienced by one exoneree after having received his compensation: "*I had a lot of people harassing me when they knew I had some money, I had drug dealers coming here ... I wouldn't buy drugs and so then they got kids to smash my car up*". The situation in the US is even more concerning. Here, nearly 50% of states do not offer any compensation for exonerees, and of those that do, some, such as Florida, do not compensate victims if they have a prior conviction of any sort (Clow et al, 2012: 329).

Despite the financial harms associated with being a victim of a miscarriage, arguably no amount of money makes it possible to return to the position that one was in prior to being wrongly convicted. Careers have been destroyed and opportunities forever lost (Bernhard, 1999). For those who have been exonerated for child sexual abuse offences, returning to employment, particularly if this involves working closely with children, may be impossible because, as a campaigner in the author's research stated, *"People believe that you can be wrongly convicted of murder, but with child abuse, it's different"*. More generally, a lack of meaningful job training while in prison and the aforementioned psychological harms that they may have suffered may combine to make exonerees unsuitable candidates for many positions (Cole, 2009). So, how might these and other harms suffered by exonerees, be addressed?

Addressing the harms caused to victims of wrongful conviction

As previously mentioned, despite the harms caused by miscarriages, the support available to help victims is minimal. The government-funded Miscarriage of Justice Support Service (MJSS), run from the Citizens Advice Bureau at the Royal Courts of Justice, offers some advice and assistance with practical tasks such as opening a bank account and applying for National Insurance credits. However, it offers no counselling or specialist assessment of victims' needs upon release (Tan, 2010). Importantly, research suggests that because the MJSS is unable to adequately meet the needs of many victims, few ultimately utilise it (Tan, 2010). The Miscarriage of Justice Organisation (MOJO), founded by Paddy Hill (an exoneree himself) and run by volunteers, also offers some practical help for victims to relearn life skills and provides emotional support (Mole, 2012). Other victims of miscarriages have also offered help in terms of providing recently released individuals with temporary accommodation at their own houses to avoid them being homeless (Jenkins, 2013a).

The small amount of research conducted in this area suggests that many victims of miscarriages require much more structured care and support than is currently provided in order to have any hope of rebuilding their lives upon release from prison. It is argued that one of the needs of the wrongly convicted is a pre-release prison plan (Tan, 2010). *Guilty* prisoners have a release programme in place, which includes, for example, training, education, counselling for release, a graded exit from the prison system through time spent in an open prison with a regime reflecting life 'outside' and home visits to help them prepare for life after prison (Tan, 2010). Due to issues mentioned previously concerning denial of 'their offence', the wrongly convicted cannot progress through the prison system or take advantage of opportunities associated with preparation for release (Westervelt and Cook, 2013). Not knowing their release date (they are usually given just a few hours' notice that their incarceration is ending), they cannot prepare themselves for life after prison in any meaningful way. Despite this, research suggests that what is needed is the provision of an intermediary stage for the wrongly convicted, similar to that offered to guilty prisoners due for release – one that allows a gradual transition from prison to freedom and that provides counselling on issues that they may experience (Mole, 2012).

When they are released, unlike the rightly convicted, who have ongoing support from probation services, the wrongly convicted have no 'go-to' person (Naughton, 2013). The multiple harms of miscarriages revealed by research highlight that this is a multidisciplinary problem (Laville, 2011). Therefore, arguably, a specific, substantial state-funded aftercare programme that pools together services provided by many different agencies and that begins the moment exonerees are released is required (Taylor and Wood, 1999). An independent residential facility where victims can receive ongoing advice, assessment and specialist treatment for specific conditions, long-term counselling to help them with traumatic memories and issues relating to displacement, and help with social and family reintegration is also required (Naughton, 2007). However, addressing the harms experienced by exonerees is not enough as they are not the only victims of miscarriages of justice.

The impact of miscarriages of justice upon victims' families

> if some moments … are spent considering the last 44 years
> of Iris Bentley's life, a much wider definition of 'victim of
> crime' becomes apparent. (Hobbs, 1997)

This statement, made in relation to the sister of Derek Bentley, who was wrongly convicted and hanged in 1952, highlights that miscarriages of justice may impact not only directly on the individual who has been wrongly convicted, but also indirectly upon individuals such as the prisoner's family. There is little research in this area. What there is suggests that while each family member is, of course, different, the impacts are significant, wide-ranging and irreversible (Innocent, no date). Indeed, as an exoneree's wife in the author's research outlined: "*When it's over, no one can get back on track. The family has broken up and it's still there.... Why did they do this to us?"*. Research suggests that family life is permanently altered as a result of a close family member being wrongly imprisoned and, indeed, that this has a 'domino effect' upon future generations (Salman, 2013). Wrongful convictions can serve to split family allegiances, as the sister of an exoneree highlighted: *"There is ... friction with my aunties ... they don't care enough ... my mother fell out with them"*. For similar reasons, the families of exonerees may see relationships suffer with close friends. For example, one woman whose son had been wrongly convicted described how she fell out with members of her church:

> I got up at chapel one Sunday and ... said 'You all sit here ... with your best hats on ... what none of you ... realise is that someone could say that your boy was seen coming out of somewhere and ... he could be picked up.... You are all praising someone who died years ago under an injustice ... but things haven't changed'.

Research has found that events associated with the wrongful conviction and imprisonment of their family member are key causes of family structures irrevocably breaking up (Westervelt and Cook, 2012). Rather ironically, while many families suffer for devoting their lives to campaigning to free their wrongly convicted relative, their release often results in them experiencing extreme difficulties in (re)building a relationship with the individual (Vollertson, 2012). Indeed, many find themselves divorced/estranged from their partner within two years of their release (Jenkins, 2013a).

Further impacts include the financial costs to families relating to, for example, loss of income due to the imprisonment of the wrongly convicted individual, money spent on attempts to contest the conviction beyond the appeal stage and establishing/running a family campaign (Jenkins, 2013a). However, the psychological impacts are arguably equally damaging. Research has revealed that the spouses, partners and children of exonerees may suffer long-term traumatic episodes associated with PTSD for years after their release (Jenkins, 2013a) and other physical and psychological difficulties such as anxiety, depression, eating disorders, regression, withdrawal, nervous breakdowns and suicidal thoughts (Cole, 2009). Children seem to fare particularly badly, with many suffering from behavioural problems, performing poorly in school and sometimes committing petty crime (Jenkins, 2014). Many report being bullied at school and becoming detached from their peers, either through withdrawal or because they are excluded from friendship groups (Grounds, 2005). Interestingly, however, as a result of old friendships breaking down, some child and adult family members form new ones by joining groups campaigning against miscarriages (Jenkins, 2013b). For many, such friendships provide the only form of psychological and/or emotional support that is often so very much needed (Jenkins, 2014).

One of the most striking impacts upon family members is the anger that they experience, both while their wrongly convicted relative is imprisoned and after their release (Naughton, 2007). As the mother of one exoneree put it to the author: "*I ... get so angry.... Why should these people who have lied live in comfort for the rest of their days.... I ... get so worked up that I want to spit*". Perhaps understandably, an unseen harm felt by many families is their loss of trust in the CJS, as the sister of an exoneree outlined: "*It has turned me against the system.... I would not trust any police officer any more*".

In addition to the aforementioned harms, many families also experience high levels of social disapproval or stigma for being connected to/supporting the victim of the wrongful conviction. This often occurs both while the individual is imprisoned and after their exoneration (Jenkins, 2014). Community reactions range from distancing themselves from the victim's family, to harassing them, to physical attempts to remove them from the community, as the sister of an exoneree in the author's research described: "*We started getting attacks on our property ... my house was firebombed*". Another interviewee described how she was asked to resign from a voluntary role that she had undertaken within the community for 10 years due to her partner's (wrongful) conviction: "*I was told that people would recognise me from the newspapers and that my colleagues would be in danger*".

Before ending this analysis of the harms caused to families, we must acknowledge the experiences of entities who are rarely mentioned in such discussions, namely, the victim/family of the victim of the original crime. When a successful appeal is announced, these individuals, who may have begun the path to recovery, are returned, without warning, to the position of 'not knowing' what happened in relation to the crime, alongside a feeling that the perpetrator (who, in their view, may or may not be the exoneree) may have escaped justice (Jenkins, 2014). As has been highlighted by the campaign group 'Justice for the 21', run by relatives of the 21 victims of the Irish Republican Army (IRA) pub bombings in Birmingham (for which the Birmingham Six were wrongly convicted), the harms engendered by decades of not knowing who killed their relatives are enduring (Lockley, 2014).

Linked to the aforementioned issue is that when, in such situations, the real perpetrators of offences are not brought to justice, other indirect victims of miscarriages may be created (Walker, 1999). Acker (2012), for example, pinpointed the new round of victimisations made in 20 wrongful conviction cases where the true perpetrators of offences remained at large. These victimisations included numerous acts of violence that had irreparable consequences for the victims involved. In their analysis of data gathered from the Innocence Project in the US, Baumgartner et al (2014) also found that of the first 300 victims of miscarriages exonerated through DNA testing since 1992, the true perpetrator was later identified in just over 50% of those cases; 130 of these perpetrators were later convicted of 139 additional violent crimes, including 33 murders and 76 sexual assaults. What of the 50% of cases where the true perpetrator was never found? There is clearly a dark figure of victimisation here, with many more victims of one miscarriage than we can ever fully be aware of.

The impact of miscarriages of justice upon the criminal justice system

Interestingly, the CJS itself may be viewed as a victim of miscarriages of justice, thereby supporting claims within victimological literature that victims and offenders are often one and the same (Miller, 2005). As previously mentioned, as a result of their experiences, direct and indirect victims of miscarriages may lose trust in the police specifically and the CJS more generally. This feeling may percolate outwards to the communities within which these victims live and may ultimately result in large numbers of people losing confidence in the CJS (Poyser, 2012). This may, in turn, reduce community cooperation with the CJS in terms of, for example, individuals' willingness to come forward as witnesses of crime. As the success of most criminal investigations relies upon information provided by the latter (see Chapter Four), this situation may dramatically reduce the number of convictions achieved by, and therefore the effectiveness of, the CJS (Poyser and Milne, 2011). The exposure of miscarriages of justice more generally may perpetrate cynical views about the CJS in otherwise law–abiding citizens, thereby calling its very legitimacy into question (Nobles and Schiff, 2000). Indeed, arguably, it is not in the system's interests to uncover many miscarriages as this may perversely lead to a drop in public confidence in the CJS (Poyser, 2012). Interestingly, over the years, some senior judges have criticised journalistic investigations into alleged miscarriages of justice on just this point, arguing that an 'insidious by-product' of media revelation of miscarriages is that it diminishes public confidence in the administration of justice (Jessell, 1994: 49). Building upon this argument, in some US states, statutes of limitation of six months or less are in place on newly discovered evidence of innocence motions because prosecutors view the revelation of a miscarriage as a 'direct attack' on the CJS (Simon and Blaskovich, 2007: 53). Perhaps, as miscarriages commentators have argued, the CJS can 'only afford ... truth ... now and then' (Woffinden, 1987: 321).

The impact of miscarriages of justice upon society

Arguably, society itself is a victim of every miscarriage of justice that occurs. Society is, for example, a victim of the significant financial costs associated with imprisoning the wrong people. As previously mentioned, those who maintain their innocence while in prison are excluded from conventional routes of making progress to parole. This means that they usually serve sentences beyond their original tariff, thereby costing the prison system and the taxpayer more money (Tan, 2010). Other costs include those incurred in relation to: the benefits system, through paying families whose major breadwinner may have been removed from the household; overturning the conviction, through drawing upon legal aid funds; the running of the publicly funded Criminal Cases Review Commission (CCRC); setting up extra-judicial inquiries; compensation paid to qualifying victims; victims suing the state/other bodies; and prosecutions relating to alleged wrongdoings (Newby, 2015).

Society may also be a victim of miscarriages of justice through their cultural impacts. Cole (2009) suggests that particularly high-profile miscarriages can harm a society's culture in that they may create widespread false beliefs about the nature, scale and types of crime committed, and by whom. This may, in turn, drive governments to enact particular crime policies without foundation. Referring to numerous wrongful convictions associated with cases of organised ritual satanic child abuse in the US in the 1980s and 1990s, Cole (2009: 438) argues that until these were revealed as miscarriages, they fuelled the cultural perception of a satanic abuse epidemic for nearly a decade, altering 'the very fabric of what [people] believed about the nature and prevalence of crime'.[1] More worryingly, they also diverted public and political attention away from the very real problems of child abuse and neglect more generally across the country. The revelation of wrongful convictions in these cases seemed to dispel such beliefs. However, the question remains as to whether unexposed miscarriages are currently shaping public conceptions of crime in many ways and ultimately affecting the version of reality that we live in (Hacking, 1995). When combined with the idea that, as Brandon and Davies (1973: 22) claim, there 'may well be certain types of wrongful conviction that are as yet not detected at any stage' of the justice process, this is a most disconcerting prospect and is just one way in which we are *all* victims of miscarriages of justice.

Conclusion

When the convictions of the Bridgewater Three were quashed in 1997, the mother of Michael Hickey asserted: 'In acquitting these ... men ... they have completed only half the task' (Anne Whelan, cited in Naughton, 2007: 169). Despite the enduring harms caused by miscarriages of justice, particularly to the wrongly convicted themselves, at present, state responsibility for these individuals ends with the quashing of the conviction (and, in a few cases, with the awarding of compensation). Wider needs concerning redress, restitution and restoration of dignity are not considered to be the duty of this particular offender (Walker and McCartney, 2008: 205). The state provides little to help the wrongly convicted cope with, and have some chance of rebuilding, their lives after exoneration and no support to their families (Grounds, 2005). The situation remains today that:

> If you are a victim of war ... or disaster ... all kinds of organisations ... will help ... if you are a victim of [the CJS] ... traumatised in a similar manner, there are few mechanisms in place to help. (Riccardelli et al, 2012: 1440)

It is imperative that further research be conducted into the array of victims of miscarriages of justice and the harms that they sustain. Empirical data on the impact of miscarriages provided by such research may, in particular, serve to further strengthen calls for changes to the conditions and circumstances into which the wrongly convicted are released. This is crucial because the little research that has been conducted to date has not influenced policy and practice in any significant way. Spotlighting the needs of exonerees and their families will, at the very least, serve to make them more 'visible victims' who, at a period in our history when the powerful are keen to highlight the elevated status of victims, deserve recognition alongside others who have suffered (Taylor and Wood, 1999: 262). Arguably, if we are genuinely committed to the notion of 'justice for all' and of 'putting victims at the heart of the justice system', we must move away from a 'one-dimensional' kind of victimology and acknowledge *all* victims, including those who are victims *of* that system.

Questions for further consideration

1. Research has revealed a number of harms caused by miscarriages of justice. However, to date, it has not examined how miscarriages might harm criminal justice practitioners themselves. Can you think of ways in which miscarriages might harm these individuals?

2. The harms of miscarriages of justice are far-reaching and long-lasting. However, little progress had been made in terms of responding to those harms. Why do you think this might be?

3. Does the government/criminal justice response to the harms of miscarriages of justice need to be costly? Are there any relatively inexpensive ways in which we might respond to them?

Note

[1] The UK has its own example in the 'satanic (child abuse) panic' of the 1990s. This led to children being removed from their homes by police in dawn raids in parts of Britain amid a climate of what Martin (2006) called 'hysteria [sweeping] through our social services'.

SIX

Formal remedies

Angus Nurse

Introduction

This chapter examines formal remedies existing for miscarriages of justice. Until the 1990s, there was limited scope for appeal against criminal conviction in England and Wales. Attempts to introduce an appellate court were continually rejected until the Court of Appeal was formally established in 1857, with a primarily civil jurisdiction, and the Court of Criminal Appeal was created in 1907 (see Chapter Two). The Court of Appeal's jurisdiction over criminal appeals was formalised by the Criminal Appeal Act 1968, when it replaced the Court of Criminal Appeal (Slapper and Kelly, 2012: 249). The 1968 Act set rules for appeal against conviction in cases where a conviction was considered unsafe, much the same as the current position, although the scope for investigation post-appeal was limited prior to 1997. As this chapter demonstrates, considerable criticism has been made of the Court of Appeal's role and performance. During the early 1990s, the perception that this had resulted in a fall in public confidence in the CJS, in part, led to calls for the creation of an independent non-judicial body that, once the standard appeal channels had been exhausted, might still investigate cases and refer them back to appeal. This institution, the Criminal Cases Review Commission (CCRC), began its work in 1997 following the Royal Commission on Criminal Procedure's (RCCP's) recommendations, which resulted in the Criminal Appeal Act 1995. The RCCP recommended that there should be a new independent authority with a remit to consider allegations of miscarriage of justice. Where there are reasons to consider that a miscarriage has occurred, the new authority, which should be independent of the police and the court structure, should be able to refer cases to the Court of Appeal. However, the CCRC (which became the new authority) has been accused of being 'not fit for purpose' and of failing to fulfil its original promise (Laville, 2012; Naughton, 2012), an allegation that this chapter assesses.

Zdenkowski (1993: 105) identifies that a number of problems exist in seeking remedies for miscarriages of justice, which are not confined to remedying wrongful imprisonment, albeit that this aspect of miscarriages arguably constitutes the most serious harm.[1] The 'wrong' to be remedied can include:

> wrongful conviction (without imprisonment); excessive punishment in terms of sanction and quantum conditions (in respect of persons properly convicted); controversy as to criminalisation of conduct (i.e. offence definition issue); improper exercise of prosecutorial discretion; and lack of adequate legal representation by reason of indigence. (Zdenkowski, 1993: 105)

Thus, the injustice requiring a remedy can be either narrow or broad and may incorporate a variety of factors. However, media, academic and policy discourse around miscarriages focuses primarily on erroneous conviction of the innocent and debates around innocence rather than the safety of conviction (Naughton, 2012).

In principle, a straightforward formal remedy for miscarriages exists in the form of appellate court scrutiny of the original trial decision: 'There are the informal agencies which can be very influential in provoking a formal review rather than conducting one' (Zdenkowski, 1993: 107), which can include media and campaigning organisations that can ultimately result in a conviction being quashed. However, the existence of formal mechanisms is integral both to making amends to the person wronged, and in identifying punitive measures against those responsible for miscarriages. Formal remedies may also identify the need for reform of criminal justice practices to eliminate sources of miscarriages or at least reduce their recurrence (Knoops, 2013). Formal remedies may therefore have direct effect, in respect of addressing the victim's harm, but can also have indirect effect, by leading to reform of criminal justice system (CJS) processes and institutions. This chapter primarily explores the extent to which the traditional appellate court approach and other mechanisms such as the CCRC provide direct redress for victims of miscarriages of justice.

The Court of Appeal

Appeals are an integral part of any justice system, acknowledging that things can and do go wrong in criminal trials, and requiring formal mechanisms through which faults in the trial process can be scrutinised and, hopefully, remedied. In criminal cases in England and Wales, there may be an appeal against conviction or sentence by the defendant, as well as a reference to the Court of Appeal by the Attorney General against a sentence that is considered to be unduly lenient in more serious cases. Those convicted of a criminal offence in the Magistrates' Court have an automatic right of appeal,[2] whereas those convicted at Crown Court need leave from the Court of Appeal. Section 2(1) of the Criminal Appeal Act 1995 provides that the Court shall allow an appeal against conviction if they think that the conviction is 'unsafe'. However, the question of what constitutes an 'unsafe' conviction is one that could doubtless be debated by scholars and practitioners *ad nauseam*. No clear statutory definition of 'unsafe' is provided (Roberts, S., 2003). However, the term 'unsafe' arguably conceptualises a multitude of sins in the trial process, ranging from doubt about the defendant's guilt, by way of error or irregularity of procedure (eg wrongful admission or exclusion of evidence), through to defects in indictment or the irregularity or wrongfulness of the verdict. At its most basic level, an unsafe conviction is one in which there may be 'lingering doubt' as to the safety of the conviction, as Lord Bingham explained in *R v Graham* [1997] 1 Cr App R 302:

> [I]f the court is satisfied, despite any misdirection of law or any irregularity in the conduct of the trial or any fresh evidence, that the conviction is safe, the court will dismiss the appeal. But if, for whatever reason, the court concludes that the appellant was wrongly convicted of the offence charged, or is left in doubt whether the appellant was rightly convicted of that offence or not, then it must of necessity consider the conviction unsafe. (Cited at para 7 of *R v Johnson and Others* [2016] EWCA Crim 1613)

The question then becomes one of *how* the Court of Appeal should examine the safety of convictions. Kerr (2013), in attempting to identify a suitable 'test' for an appellate court to apply in quashing a conviction, referred to Lord Hope's judgment in *McInnes v Her Majesty's Advocate* [2010] UKSC 7, 2010 SC (UKSC) 28.[3] At paragraph 24, Lord Hope said:

> The test which [the Lord Justice-General] identified was whether there was a real risk of prejudice to the defence. These remarks, I would respectfully suggest, need some explanation. They invite questions as to how robust the test

must be and how the real risk is to be identified. They need to be taken just one step further to indicate more precisely the test that should be applied. The question which lies at the heart of it is one of fairness. The question which the appeal court must ask itself is whether after taking full account of all the circumstances of the trial, including the non-disclosure in breach of the appellant's Convention right, the jury's verdict should be allowed to stand. That question will be answered in the negative if there was a real possibility of a different outcome – if the jury might reasonably have come to a different view on the issue to which it directed its verdict if the withheld material had been disclosed to the defence.

Unsafe convictions may, therefore, combine both 'innocence' appeals, where the crux of the issue is a concern that an innocent defendant has been convicted, and 'due process' appeals, where innocence may not directly be at issue, but doubts exist concerning the safety of the *process*. This raises particular concern where procedural fault has arguably facilitated the jury's consideration towards guilt. The Court of Appeal has, however, clarified that:

> This court is not concerned with guilt or innocence of the appellants, but only with the safety of their convictions. This may at first sight, appear an unsatisfactory state of affairs, until it is remembered that the integrity of the criminal process is the most important consideration for courts which have to hear appeals against conviction. Both the innocent and the guilty are entitled to fair trials. If the trial process is not fair, if it is distorted by deceit or material breaches of the rules of evidence or procedure, then the liberties of all are threatened. (McConville and Marsh, 2014: 58)

Concerns that appeals are decided on technical grounds are not new, with Orfield, for example, highlighting in 1937 that reversing a conviction on technical grounds arguably offered 'one more loophole for the criminal' (Orfield, 1937: 668). Quirk (2007: 760) identifies that in 2006, the government published a consultation 'on changing the appellate test so that the "guilty" will not have their convictions quashed on the basis of legal or procedural errors'. However, as with other areas of miscarriage of justice remedies, the Court of Appeal's jurisprudence demonstrates that innocence is not the sole consideration. In *R v*

Davis, Rowe and Johnson [2001] 1 Cr App R 8, the court confirmed that 'a conviction may be unsafe even where there is no doubt about guilt but the trial process has been vitiated by serious unfairness or significant legal misdirection'. Thus, the Court of Appeal serves largely as a review of procedural correctness and fairness at trial (Quirk, 2007: 763), including whether material fault in the trial process or other error might dictate that an individual has been denied their right to a fair trial, as guaranteed by Article 6 of the European Convention on Human Rights (ECHR).[4] Zellick (2010: 14) argues that by studying the jurisprudence of the Court of Appeal, it is possible to construct five categories of unsafe convictions, as follows:

- First, and foremost, new evidence that, had it been before the jury, might have produced a different verdict.
- Second, the identification of procedural or other irregularity or mistake of law that leaves a doubt about whether the jury's verdict would have been the same without the error.
- Third, a serious irregularity constituting an abuse of process or resulting in a trial falling short of the basic standards of fairness, which may well cover unfairness contrary to Article 6 of the ECHR.
- Fourth, that there remains a 'lurking doubt' about the safety (soundness) of the conviction.
- Fifth, where case law has changed to the defendant's advantage since the date of the conviction, in the light of which the conviction now appears unsafe (see also Chapter Three).[5]

Thus, the Court of Appeal is arguably engaged more in conducting due process appeals than innocence appeals, although such due process appeals have been under attack for some time. Liberty (2006: 4–5), in responding to the consultation on 'quashing convictions', raised concerns about the possibility that:

> once the Court of Appeal's power to quash a conviction outright where there has been serious malpractice on the part of state authorities is removed, the next step will be to take that power away from the courts of first instance.

The power to stay proceedings as an abuse of process is an important constitutional safeguard that must not be restricted or removed. Quirk (2007: 760) also suggested that 'there are many reasons, pragmatic and principled, for resisting the introduction of an innocence criterion for appeals'. Notwithstanding the difficulties of actually *proving* innocence, retaining the appellate test of 'safety' brings with it important due process safeguards applicable equally to the guilty and the innocent, both of whom are entitled to protection from abuse of process. It also provides a remedy through appellate means where their rights are abused.

While the Court of Appeal provides a remedy in principle, in practice, the Court has been criticised for a restrictive and cautious approach (Nobles and Schiff, 2000: 74; George, 2015). In particular, criticisms have been raised that the Court 'is overly reluctant to interfere with a properly delivered jury verdict, requiring appellants to show some material irregularity or fresh evidence' (House of Commons Justice Committee, 2015: 13) before a conviction has any real possibility of being quashed. The Court has also been criticised for its 'atomistic' approach of considering fresh material in an isolated fashion rather than reviewing the whole picture in a case. There have also been concerns of inconsistency in the Court's jurisprudence, creating difficulties for the CCRC (discussed further later) in predicting the Court's approach (House of Commons Justice Committee, 2015: 13–15).

Human rights claims

Separate from the traditional appellate court route, a potential remedy for miscarriages of justice and wrongful convictions arising from deficiencies in the fairness of a trial exist on human rights grounds. Article 6 of the ECHR sets out the following rights:

- Everyone is entitled to a fair and public hearing within a reasonable time
- Everyone charged with a criminal offence shall be presumed innocent until proved guilty according to law
- Everyone charged with a criminal offence has the following minimum rights:
  a) to be informed promptly, in a language which he understands and in detail, of the nature and cause of the accusation against him;
  b) to have adequate time and facilities for the preparation of his defence;
  c) to defend himself in person or through legal assistance of his own choosing or, if he has not sufficient means to pay for legal assistance, to be given it free when the interests of justice so require;

d) to examine or have examined witnesses against him and to obtain the attendance and examination of witnesses on his behalf under the same conditions as witnesses against him;

e) to have the free assistance of an interpreter if he cannot understand or speak the language used in court.

The nature of the ECHR Article 6 rights is such that a breach of these may well lead to a wrongful conviction and thus a miscarriage of justice according to this book's definition. Where a defendant has been denied a fair trial or the opportunity to put forward a robust defence has been compromised, Section 7 of the Human Rights Act 1998 offers a number of possible remedies. Section 7(1)(a) provides for the right to bring proceedings against a public authority while section 7(1)(b) contains the right to rely on the ECHR in any legal proceedings against a public authority (Wadham and Mountfield, 1999: 38–51).

The Human Rights Act 1998 allows a victim of human rights breaches to bring various claims against state criminal justice agencies.[6] A victim may bring claims that a public body has acted or proposes to act in a way that would be unlawful by not being human-rights-compliant. Alternatively, claims may be pursued concerning some form of flaw in the criminal justice process that denies a victim their human rights, for example, the exclusion of evidence, unfair trial, abuse of process or that criminal justice action was arbitrary or disproportionate. Claims might also be brought that the state has unnecessarily interfered with citizens' private lives, that the state has failed to safeguard or has had disregard for the lives of its citizens, and that action by the state amounts to cruel and unusual punishment. The Human Rights Act 1998 applies to the police service as a public authority, against which human rights complaints can now be made within UK courts (Neyroud and Beckley, 2001: 63). Arguably, the ECHR has had a significant impact on policing (Neyroud, 2008: 99), with Patten (1999: 18) going as far as to suggest that the ECHR has redefined the nature of policing as the 'protecting of human rights'. Human rights considerations must also be applied to the Crown Prosecution Service (CPS) as a public body and also to the courts. Thus, a victim of abuse of process or failings in the trial process need not rely solely on the traditional appellate route regarding an 'unsafe' conviction; they may bring human rights claims to address aspects of an alleged miscarriage.

However, human rights claims need not be separate from appellate procedures and can be part of an appeal, particularly in respect of alleged failings in the collection of evidence used at trial, for example, illegal surveillance and confessions (see Chapters Three and Four). Appeals may well bring into consideration issues where UK law has allegedly been misapplied or is in conflict with European human rights law (see the case study later in this chapter). Appeals may also identify where criminal justice agencies have failed in the required positive duty to uphold convention rights and protect life and other rights, such as private and family life (Neyroud and Beckley, 2001: 68). Arguably, the Human Rights Act 1998 expands the remedies available to a victim of a miscarriage or at least the grounds on which challenges to the safety of a conviction might be pursued. Where appellate mechanisms have failed or been exhausted and where new evidence arises that casts doubt upon the soundness of decisions arising from the original trial, there may be recourse to the CCRC.

The Criminal Cases Review Commission

The CCRC was established on 1 January 1997 and is responsible for examining suspected miscarriages of justice in England, Wales and Northern Ireland. The CCRC:

> cannot overturn convictions or sentences itself. Instead it may refer to the Court of Appeal a conviction for an offence tried on indictment, or a finding of not guilty by reason of insanity, or a finding that a person was under a disability when he did the act or made the omission, and may also refer cases in respect of sentence where they were tried on indictment. (Slapper and Kelly, 2012: 260)

The CCRC's jurisdiction under the Criminal Appeal Act 1995 means that, in practical terms, it is not seeking to establish innocence, even though this may be a by-product of its actions. The Criminal Appeal Act 1995 requires that only cases with the 'real possibility' of the conviction being overturned should be referred to the Court of Appeal. Thus, the CCRC will be selective in those cases that it refers to the Court of Appeal, but, in this regard, it is no different from any other investigative or quasi-judicial body, all of whom reach judgements on what cases they will or will not pursue and the criteria by which matters within their jurisdiction will be determined. One principle of quasi-judicial bodies like the CCRC is that they are generally granted discretion over how they exercise their judgement, and providing that they do so in a logical manner and give reasons for their decisions, there is no reason why they should not do so (Nurse, 2012). Criticisms over the way that the CCRC decides which cases to refer are thus arguably criticisms of the decision itself, not the actual function, and while there will inevitably be those who disagree with specific decisions, it is the role of the CCRC once entrusted with the discretion to decide how to exercise it.

The courts have upheld the CCRC's independence in a range of decisions concerning such quasi-judicial bodies, as has the House of Commons Justice Committee (2015). In *Re Fletcher's Application* [1970] 2 All ER 527, the courts refused to grant an order requiring the Parliamentary Commissioner to investigate an allegation of neglect of duty against the Official Receiver. The House of Lords concluded that the courts had no jurisdiction to order the Commissioner to carry out an investigation. The administrative law principle at stake is that quasi-judicial commissions and Commissioners must be free to exercise their functions as they see fit. In *R v The CCRC, ex parte Pearson* [1999] EWHC (Admin) 452 [2000], Lord Bingham reinforced this view, making clear that the decision on whether or not to refer a case to the Court of Appeal 'lay fairly and squarely within the area of judgment entrusted to the Commission' and concluded that if the court were to assess the merits of the CCRC's judgement, 'it would be exceeding its role'. In *Morris v the CCRC* [2011] EHHC 117, the High Court reiterated this view. The Court held that as the CCRC is vested with the power and duty to assess which cases cross the threshold for a reference to the Court of Appeal and which do not, it is not for the courts to scrutinise cases where an individual, no matter how much they are rightly aggrieved, wishes to challenge the CCRC's 'evaluative' judgements.

Criticism of the Criminal Cases Review Commission

In *R (on the application of Nunn) (Appellant) v Chief Constable of Suffolk Constabulary and another (Respondents)* [2014] UKSC 37, the Supreme Court explained the CCRC's role and powers as follows:

> in response to the recommendations of the Runciman Commission, the law of England and Wales (and also of Northern Ireland and Scotland) has put in place a separate body, the Criminal Cases Review Commission ('CCRC'), which has the power to review any conviction and which is charged, if it thinks that there is a real possibility that the Court of Appeal might quash the conviction, with the power to refer the case back to that court for, exceptionally,

the hearing of a second appeal – and on any grounds, whether the same as before or different. Such a referral bypasses the requirement for leave to appeal. An arguable case is assumed. The Court thereupon has the duty to investigate the safety of the conviction and must quash it if it is unsafe. The CCRC's extensive investigative powers include the power to require the production to it of any material in the hands of the police or any other public body, to appoint an investigator with all the powers of a police officer, and to assemble fresh evidence not before the court of trial.

The CCRC thus has wide-ranging investigative powers, although, in practice, it is primarily concerned with investigating with a view to determining whether there is a 'real possibility' of a conviction being quashed, which arguably limits the extent to which cases are referred to the Court of Appeal (discussed further in the following and in Chapter Seven).

Critics of the CCRC point to various factors in determining that the organisation has 'failed'. Journalist Bob Woffinden (2010) described it as little more than a fig leaf and with a dubious record of success; others argue that it does little to help the innocent who are wrongly convicted. While the CCRC has arguably achieved limited success in quashing major convictions, its very existence (acknowledged by Woffinden and others to be unique) should be celebrated. Few jurisdictions have a body that *routinely* examines the cases of those who feel that they have been wrongly convicted or unfairly sentenced, and that provides free access to aggrieved citizens and a formal review mechanism without the need to involve lawyers.

In reality, the CCRC's role is not to establish the innocence of those making applications to it, but instead to examine, with a view to establishing the safety or otherwise of, convictions in the cases brought before it (Jessel, 2009). This involves independent review of procedural and evidential faults that cause the innocent to be convicted on a case-by-case basis. The focus on the safety of the conviction is integral to the CCRC's jurisdiction, requiring examination of cases specifically to consider whether there might have been an error that new evidence could correct or that might provide grounds for a review. It has never been the CCRC's role to decide the innocence of an individual or to establish the case for reform of the CJS. Arguably, this was the intention of campaigners, media and politicians when the CCRC was established. Naughton (2012: 210) suggests that the

CCRC 'is not the solution to the wrongful conviction of the factually innocent that it was widely thought to be'. The CCRC's creation in the wake of high-profile miscarriages involving defendants identified as being believed innocent carried with it the hope that the CCRC would address factual innocence rather than technical fault (Naughton, 2012). However, Innocence Commissions with a remit to assess innocence are an entirely different thing, sometimes established to provide remedies for factually innocent victims of wrongful convictions (the error-correction model) or sometimes charged with providing advice about how to reform the CJS to prevent future occurrences of wrongful conviction (the systematic reform model). The North Carolina Innocence Inquiry Commission,[7] for example, has the determination of claims of factual innocence from living persons as its remit, while the public inquiry commissions employed by Canadian provincial governments are generally appointed after a conviction has been quashed and conduct investigations into the causes of the particular wrongful convictions. However, these Canadian commissions can also make specific recommendations for changes to the CJS arising from their investigations. For example, the Commission on Proceedings Involving Guy Paul Morin, an Ontario public inquiry into a wrongful murder conviction, made specific recommendations on the use of forensic science evidence, including; the requirement for forensic opinion to be acted upon only when in writing; the establishing of a written policy and guidelines on report writing for forensic reports; the creation of an advisory board and a full quality assurance unit; the monitoring of courtroom evidence; and the training of staff. Other Canadian wrongful conviction commissions have made recommendations such as the mandatory sharing of investigation reports between all police forces assisting in major cases and guidance to trial judges on how juries should be directed to consider and weigh identification evidence (Nurse, 2012). Such recommendations seek to identify the causes of wrongful convictions and to aid the development of practices to prevent their recurrence.

The House of Commons Justice Committee (2015) recently made recommendations concerning the CCRC's role. It noted that the CCRC is performing its functions 'reasonably well', but also identified areas for improvement. In respect of the 'real possibility' test, the Committee concluded:

> We have seen no conclusive evidence that the CCRC is failing to apply the 'real possibility' test correctly in the majority of cases. We accept that application of the test is …

no means a precise science, but where potential miscarriages of justice are concerned we consider that the CCRC should be willing to err on the side of making a referral ... [and] definitely never fear disagreeing with, or being rebuked by, the Court of Appeal. (House of Commons Justice Committee, 2015: 12).

The Committee concluded that if a bolder CCRC approach leads to more failed appeals but one additional miscarriage being corrected, that would be of clear benefit (also see Chapter Seven).

Compensation for miscarriages of justice

Stephanie Roberts (2003: 441) identifies that a statutory compensation scheme for wrongful convictions is needed to comply with the UK's obligations under Article 14(6) of the International Covenant on Civil and Political Rights (ICCPR), which states that:

> When a person has by a final decision been convicted of a criminal offence and when subsequently his conviction has been reversed or he has been pardoned on the ground that a new or newly discovered fact shows conclusively that there has been a miscarriage of justice, the person who has suffered punishment as a result of such conviction shall be compensated according to law, unless it is proved that the non-disclosure of the unknown fact in time is wholly or partly attributable to him.

Compensation provisions in English law are to be found in Section 133 of the Criminal Justice Act 1988 ('the 1988 Act'), as amended by the Anti-Social Behaviour, Crime and Policing Act 2014 ('the 2014 Act'). Section 133(1), as originally constituted, broadly replicates Article 14(6) of the ICCPR and provides a framework for the secretary of state to:

> pay compensation for the miscarriage of justice to the person who has suffered punishment as a result of such conviction or, if he is dead, to his personal representatives, unless the non-disclosure of the unknown fact was wholly or partly attributable to the person convicted.

The amendment introduced by the 2014 Act inserts a new Section 133(1ZA) into the 1988 Act, which defines 'miscarriage of justice' as follows:

> For the purpose of subsection (1), there has been a miscarriage of justice in relation to a person convicted of a criminal offence in England and Wales or, in a case where subsection 6H applies, Northern Ireland, if and only if the new or newly discovered fact shows beyond reasonable doubt that the person did not commit the offence (and references in the rest of this Part to a miscarriage of justice are to be construed accordingly).

Arguably, this amendment limits the paying of compensation to those circumstances where an individual has been declared 'innocent', although the government's own online guidance (available at https://www.gov.uk/claim-compensation-for-miscarriage-of-justice) identifies that compensation can be claimed if a conviction has been overturned (or quashed) by the courts and *any* of the following apply:

- your appeal was successful and it was submitted 28 days or more after your conviction, or 21 days or more after a conviction in a magistrates' court;
- your conviction was overturned after it was referred to the Court of Appeal by the CCRC; and
- you have been granted a free pardon.

In 2011, the Supreme Court was asked to determine what the phrase 'miscarriage of justice' meant in respect of the statutory compensation scheme. In *R (Adams) v Secretary of State for Justice* [2011] UKSC 18, the Supreme Court identified that the phrase was capable of having different meanings. For the purposes of the compensation scheme, the Supreme Court determined that the rules should not be restricted to applicants who are able to conclusively demonstrate their innocence. Instead, it should be extended to cases where a new or newly discovered fact 'so undermines the evidence against the defendant that no conviction could possibly be based upon it'.

However, the government 'has since legislated to reverse the effect of this decision' (Lipscombe and Beard, 2015: 1), so that for applications made on or after 13 March 2014, there will have been a miscarriage of justice 'if and only if the new or newly discovered fact shows beyond reasonable doubt that the person did not commit the offence'.[8] Thus, payment of compensation is now arguably linked to determination of innocence, which, as this chapter indicates, is rarely the concern of appellate mechanisms, and arguably should not be given the reality that determining actual innocence is acknowledged as being difficult and something that the Court of Appeal has expressly said is not its role.

Under the current scheme, if the secretary of state decides that an applicant is eligible for compensation under Section 133, the question of how much should be awarded is determined by an independent assessor. The secretary of state can make deductions for any conduct of the applicant that contributed to the conviction, for his criminal record and for 'saved living expenses'. The maximum amount of compensation payable is £1 million in cases where the applicant has been imprisoned for at least 10 years, or £500,000 in all other cases. Lipscombe and Beard (2015: 1) note that while it might be assumed that victims of miscarriages of justice must be entitled to compensation, particularly if they have spent time in custody before being pardoned or having their convictions quashed, 'compensation is the exception rather than the rule'.

Case study: *R (Hallam and Nealon) v Secretary of State for Justice* [2016] EWCA Civ 355

Hallam was imprisoned at age 17 and convicted of murder. His murder conviction was later quashed by the Court of Appeal but he had already spent seven and a half years in custody. His application for compensation was rejected. He judicially reviewed that decision, arguing that the new legislation governing compensation (s.133(1ZA) of the Criminal Justice Act 1988) was unlawful as it was contrary to the presumption of innocence within Article 6(2) of the ECHR. He sought a declaration of incompatibility under the Human Rights Act 1998. As it raised similar issues of law, his claim was joined to a similar claim by Victor Nealon.

In *R (Adams) v Secretary of State for Justice* [2012] UKSC 18, a majority of the Supreme Court found that:

> while the presumption of innocence guaranteed by article 6.2 of the Convention prevented a state from undermining the effect of a criminal acquittal, the procedure enacted by section 133 of the 1988 Act providing for the decision on entitlement to compensation to be taken by the executive was separate and raised different questions from the proceedings in a criminal court, and the refusal of compensation on the basis that the claimant has not proved beyond reasonable doubt that a miscarriage of justice had occurred would not infringe Article 6.2.

The Court of Appeal rejected the secretary of state's argument that Article 6(2) does not apply to applications for compensation for miscarriage of justice. However, the Court of Appeal considered that it was bound by previous Supreme Court authority to conclude, contrary to a more recent Strasbourg authority, that Article 6(2) did not apply. The Court of Appeal also decided that the terms of the test in Section 133(1ZA) of the Criminal Justice Act 1988 did not offend the presumption of innocence. For these reasons, it rejected the appeals by Mr Hallam and Mr Nealon. At its core, this case emphasises that the right to compensation under Section 133 of the 1988 Act does not require the claimant to prove his innocence. Instead, the secretary of state must be satisfied as to the link between the new facts and the applicant's innocence before he is required to pay compensation under the 1988 Act.

Accordingly, the Court of Appeal's dismissal of Hallam's and Nealon's appeals left them unable to claim miscarriage of justice compensation. At the time of writing, it is understood that Hallam hopes to obtain permission to appeal to the Supreme Court (Seabrook, 2016; Smith, C., 2016).

The Nealon and Hallam case illustrates the potential difficulties of obtaining compensation. As Robins (2016b) notes: 'Nealon and Hallam find themselves caught in a bind: undoubtedly innocent but, as they can't categorically demonstrate their innocence, they are not entitled for compensation for the damage done to them'. Campbell (2015) indicates that one potential implication of the new rules is that 'the Ministry of Justice is now making it virtually impossible for anyone to be compensated unless someone else is convicted of the crime'. The wording of the Court of Appeal's ruling that the secretary of state must be 'satisfied' of a clear link between the new facts and the defendant's innocence gives credence to this view.

Conclusion

In one sense, it is impossible to fully remedy a miscarriage of justice as the CJS cannot put the victim of a miscarriage back in the position that they would have been had the miscarriage not occurred. Indeed, as this chapter shows, remedies for wrongful conviction rarely lead to a declaration of innocence. Arguably, a declaration of innocence is the closest thing to nullifying the conviction while perhaps not addressing the psychological harm and lost years that result from wrongful conviction and imprisonment. However, as Robins (2016b) notes, victims themselves identify that while money cannot make up for the harm that has been done, it at least provides recognition of harm from the state. Miscarriages of justice ruin lives and undermine confidence in the CJS, and it is not enough that the state reviews only the safety of convictions, no matter how well the Court of Appeal or the CCRC does this. The state must also seek to: remedy the harm directly caused to victims of miscarriages; redress the wider harm that miscarriages cause to confidence in the CJS; and remedy the faults that miscarriages reveal within criminal justice processes (see Chapter Five).

Formal remedies for miscarriages undoubtedly exist in the appellate mechanisms that provide for those wrongly convicted to have their convictions quashed. Notwithstanding criticisms of its effectiveness, the CCRC also arguably does good work by providing for the extra-judicial review of cases that have reached the end of the road in the appellate system. The CCRC has, however, the potential to contribute further by not only resolving miscarriages of justice when they occur, but also helping policymakers and professionals to understand their causes and how to prevent them (Nurse, 2012). Theoretically, at least, there is no reason why the CCRC cannot function as both an error-correction and systematic reform commission, although this does require amendment to its jurisdiction.

At present, the CCRC rarely expresses views on legislative reform except in respect of legislation that directly affects its functions. However, there is scope to amend the Criminal Appeal Act 1995 to give the CCRC the power to make recommendations or provide guidance on the causes of miscarriages. Other quasi-judicial bodies such as the Information Commissioner and the Commission for Local Administration in England (the Local Government Ombudsman) combine their investigative functions with a duty to promote good practice. The (Local Government) Ombudsmen interpret their powers under the Local Government Act 1974 as providing a duty to provide guidance and disseminate information on what constitutes good (and bad) administration. By investigating individual complaints, the Ombudsmen may identify 'more generalised weaknesses in practices, rules and attitudes' (Seneviratne, 2000), and from investigative findings, they may identify a need for changes to administrative practices that will benefit other citizens. They disseminate this information in the form of guidance notes on good administrative practice and special reports on areas where common administrative mistakes occur. The Information Commissioner also publishes codes of practice and compliance and legal guidance. While these bodies admittedly have different jurisdictions to that of the CCRC, the provisions of their respective legislation allow them to develop and publish guidance on areas of systematic fault identified through their casework, as well as guidance on the requirements of good practice based on the failures that they uncover through their investigative work and their developing body of case law arising from this work. The CCRC is uniquely placed to do the same for miscarriages of justice given its casework experience, and to play an advisory role in the development of the CJS such that a repeat of particular miscarriages can be addressed.

Questions for further consideration

1. What difficulties exist in defining whether a conviction is 'unsafe'?

2. What criticisms have been made of the CCRC and how might these be addressed?

3. What problems exist in securing compensation for miscarriages of justice?

Notes

[1] Notwithstanding the fact that in other jurisdictions such as the US, a miscarriage can result in the execution of the innocent. The US Death Penalty Information Centre (2016: 2) states that, since 1973, more than 150 people have been released from death row with evidence of their innocence. From 1973 to 1999, an average of three exonerations occurred per year; from 2000 to 2011, there were an average of five exonerations per year.

[2] Section 108 of the Magistrates Courts Act 1980.

[3] It should be noted that this is a Scottish Case and Lord Kerr recognised the differences between Scots and English law. However, his lordship's speech noted that, in practical terms, the tests applied in England/Wales and in Scotland had the same effect, namely, to identify unsafe convictions, that is, those where a miscarriage of justice had occurred.

[4] Notwithstanding the fact that an individual so aggrieved may well invoke their ECHR rights or may seek to pursue a claim via action in UK courts under the Human Rights Act 1998 or by recourse to the European Court of Human Rights (ECtHR).

[5] See, for example, *R v Jogee* [2016] UKSC 8 and the Supreme Court's ruling that law on joint enterprise had taken a 'wrong turn in 1984' and that it was 'the responsibility of this court to put the law right'.

[6] Section 7(7) of the Human Rights Act 1998 effectively defines a 'victim' as somebody directly affected by the actions of a public authority.

7   The Commission is made up of eight members selected by the Chief Justice of the North Carolina Supreme Court and the Chief Judge of the North Carolina Court of Appeals, see: http://www.innocencecommission-nc.gov/

8   Section 175 of the Anti-Social Behaviour, Crime and Policing Act 2014.

SEVEN

Informal remedies

Sam Poyser

Introduction

> Informal remedies are needed because the ... process that
> convicts people is fallible [and] the formal mechanisms for
> reviewing convictions fail to adequately recognise this ...
> someone has to challenge the injustice perpetuated by the
> system. (Eady, 2016)

This statement, made by a veteran miscarriage of justice campaigner, provides some insight into why informal remedies are required to help rectify some miscarriages and to support those fighting such injustice. It suggests that when the pre-trial system fails, the post-trial appellate system in place to remedy miscarriages also sometimes fails to recognise and rectify them. This 'double failure of justice' is problematic as it is effectively the 'end of the line' for the wrongly imprisoned individual. The formal remedies in place, namely, the Court of Appeal and the Criminal Cases Review Commission (CCRC) have proved ineffectual, leaving victims of injustice seemingly without hope. Informal remedies, then, are often the last resort for individuals who have been failed at every stage of the criminal justice process, including the appellate system (Poyser, 2012).

Informal remedies are vital in providing support to victims. In some cases, where it is impossible to reveal the wrongful conviction, they may even provide a form of 'palliative care' (Eady, 2016) for the wrongly convicted and their family (as no formal mechanism exists to do this). Furthermore, just occasionally, informal remedies may be a significant factor in overturning a wrongful conviction. Indeed, just as many miscarriages have multiple causes, many are remedied by multiple factors, with victims dependent upon the hard work of others in helping to overturn their conviction (Poyser, 2012). These entities include campaigning organisations, journalists, Innocence projects, charitable projects and family campaigns.

This chapter will begin by briefly outlining why informal remedies are often sought by victims of miscarriages of justice. The chapter will then consider various entities involved in trying to remedy miscarriages and/or to support those who try to do so from this informal perspective, as well as the activities that they engage in. Importantly, where possible, the chapter will draw upon findings from empirical research conducted by the author. This research (see also Chapter Five) involved semi-structured interviews with a sample of individuals ($N = 39$) who had been associated with efforts to expose miscarriages of justice, either alone or as part of established campaigns. These individuals included members of various campaigning organisations, families and friends of the wrongly convicted, campaigning lawyers and journalists, and others involved in contesting convictions. The research aimed to discover the key factors that lead to success in campaigns against miscarriages – in other words, it asked 'What informal remedies work and how do they work?'. Importantly, this chapter does not discuss in any depth issues that campaigners and others have raised concerning the effectiveness of the Court of Appeal in recognising/rectifying miscarriages (see Chapter Six). However, it does highlight concerns raised by the House of Commons Justice Committee (2015) regarding the effectiveness of the CCRC (see also Chapter Six) as the most recently developed formal remedy for miscarriages. Indeed, this is how we begin the following discussion.

Why might informal remedies be required?

Chapter Six has already discussed the formal remedies available to those who claim that they have been wrongly convicted in England and Wales. Essentially, these individuals have at their disposal the appeals process consisting of primarily the Court of Appeal and CCRC. Although, as our history demonstrates, England and Wales were slow to establish a Court of Appeal in comparison to other countries (see Chapter Two), the opposite occurred in relation to the establishment of the CCRC. Beginning work in 1997, the CCRC was the first organisation of its kind and remains one of only a handful of similar bodies worldwide (Naughton, 2012). Chapter Six has detailed the functions of the CCRC and how its work relates to that of the Court of Appeal. Here, it is suffice to say that the CCRC receives applications from appellants whose previous appeals to the Court of Appeal have failed but who continue to challenge their conviction (Jenkins, 2014). The CCRC operates under various restrictions, not least limited resources. Some suggest that this means that it sometimes does not engage in the 'on-the-ground' investigative work required to discover fresh evidence in a case (O'Neill, 2011: 28). Indeed, David Jessell (CCRC Commissioner during 2000–10) suggests that its investigative 'legwork' has been reduced because it 'does not see investigating as a primary aim anymore' (cited in O'Neill, 2011: 28). Limited resources also mean that it can take several years for the CCRC to refer a case to the Court of Appeal (Jenkins, 2014). Additionally, the CCRC operates under constraints imposed upon it by the Criminal Appeals Act 1995, one of the most controversial of which surrounds the issue of 'real possibility'. As Chapter Six discusses, the CCRC examines cases where a miscarriage is alleged and decides if there is any new evidence/argument not heard at trial/an earlier appeal that raises a 'real possibility' that the Court of Appeal would quash the conviction/ reduce the sentence (Naughton, 2007). Cases are referred from the CCRC to the Court of Appeal, therefore, when they are judged to have met the 'real possibility test'. However, a problem expressed by many is that during any hearings prior to submitting an application to the CCRC, the appellant has usually already used up their new evidence/argument. This makes a fresh application to the CCRC on this basis problematic (Jenkins, 2014).

As Chapter Six outlines, in 2015, the House of Commons Justice Committee reviewed the effectiveness of the CCRC and invited Innocence project leaders, lawyers, journalists, campaigners and others involved in trying to remedy miscarriages to give evidence. Its report subsequently outlined a concern that 'there may be some miscarriages … which are going uncorrected because of the difficulty the CCRC faces in getting some such cases past the threshold of "real possibility"' (House of Commons Justice Committee, 2015: 16) and urged the Law Commission to review the Court of Appeal's grounds for allowing appeals, stating that it should:

> encourage the Court of Appeal to quash a conviction where it has a serious doubt about the verdict, *even without fresh evidence or fresh legal argument*. If any such change is made, it should be accompanied by a review of its effects on the CCRC and of the continuing appropriateness of the 'real possibility' test. (House of Commons Justice Committee, 2015: 17; emphasis added)

The response of the then Justice Minister Michael Gove was that the government would not invite the Law Commission to review the Court of Appeal's grounds for allowing appeals because 'there is [in] sufficient evidence that the ... current approach has a deleterious effect on those who have suffered a miscarriage' (cited in Price, 2016). This is just one reason why many argue that informal remedies are required as much today as they ever were.

Types of informal remedies and how they may help victims of miscarriages of justice

Concerns surrounding the CCRC's effectiveness in revealing wrongful convictions have led to many victims and their families turning to others for help (Jenkins, 2014). These 'informal remedies' serve many purposes, from providing emotional support through to attempting to reinvestigate alleged miscarriages in what some suggest is a more timely, proactive and, in some cases, successful manner than the CCRC (O'Neill, 2011: 28). However, before proceeding, we must note that if fresh evidence *is* discovered as a result of an informal investigation, those involved still cannot rectify the wrongful conviction without engaging with formal remedies. The finding of new evidence only helps the wrongly convicted person if it is accepted by the CCRC and Court of Appeal and results in the conviction being quashed. The Court of Appeal has the power to reject appeals with fresh evidence where it is believed that another explanation for the new evidence satisfies the upholding of the conviction (Poyser, 2012), and it has done so on many occasions (see Jeremy Bamber's case [BBC, 2012]). Clearly, informal remedies that seek to discover fresh evidence in a case remain bound by the limitations of the formal remedies above them as only *they* hold the power to overturn convictions. This said, informal remedies available to some victims of miscarriages are detailed in the following.

Campaigning organisations

One type of informal remedy that victims and their families may turn to when they experience a wrongful conviction is the campaigning organisation. Numerous bodies in England and Wales provide assistance to victims and their families, ranging from emotional support, through to providing physical venues for meetings, through to acting as a source of information (Jenkins, 2013b).

Additionally, they may supply victims with links to professionals such as specialist lawyers and/or expert witnesses who may be useful in their fight to expose a miscarriage. Frequently, such organisations are also involved in awareness-raising, fund-raising and lobbying. Most are positive and progressive, engaging in efforts to reform the criminal justice system (CJS) by, for example, responding to government consultations/policy. Thus, they often focus upon individual cases in addition to the broader problems exposed by those cases (Jenkins, 2013b). Most campaigning organisations have a web presence used to publicise specific cases, highlight particular issues and provide links to similar organisations.

Importantly, these organisations stress that they cannot help individuals who have been wrongly convicted on technical grounds (eg when a murder conviction should have been manslaughter) (Jenkins, 2013b). They support only those who claim to be factually innocent (Naughton, 2007), although, of course, this is usually difficult to verify. Most organisations only campaign on behalf of those wrongly convicted of serious crimes due to limited resources/time (Naughton, 2007).

Three broad types of organisation are involved in miscarriages campaigning. These include, first, large established civil liberties/ human rights bodies such as Justice, Liberty, Amnesty International and Statewatch. These bodies have different 'voices' and priorities. However, they all campaign (inter)nationally on (in)justice issues, their involvement in miscarriages being just one element of their work (Jenkins, 2014). Many of them occupy a 'watchdog role', scrutinising state/CJS activities, but they are also progressive, engaging in dialogue with the latter to try to achieve change (Jenkins, 2013b). This might include providing hard evidence to bolster calls for reform in relation to an issue being analysed by those in power. 'Justice' has been particularly influential in terms of providing evidence to major committees concerned with investigating particular causes of miscarriages. In the 1970s, for example, it provided details of 30 wrongful convictions based on mistaken identification to the Devlin Committee (Devlin, 1976) established to review the law and procedures surrounding identification parades. This led Lord Devlin to conclude that erroneous eyewitness identification evidence was a major source of miscarriages and to make recommendations (later enshrined in law) relating to the need for utmost caution to be exercised when considering the reliability of such evidence (Robins, 2014). Throughout the 1980s, Tom Sargant, the then secretary of 'Justice', also supplied the producer of a new BBC TV series, 'Rough justice', with cases of alleged wrongful conviction for him to investigate, a collaboration that resulted in several convictions being overturned (Hill et al, 1985).

The second type of organisation involved in campaigning in this area are national and regional bodies solely concerned with miscarriages of justice. Those operating nationally include Innocent, the Miscarriage of Justice Organisation (MOJO) and Miscarriages of Justice UK (MOJUK). Some of these bodies have latterly engaged in preventive work relating to individuals who fear that they *may be* wrongly convicted. Some also aid reinvestigations into cases, thereby helping to ultimately overturn wrongful convictions (Innocent, no date). Importantly, Innocent helped to set up United Against Injustice, a federation of regional groups campaigning against miscarriages, which includes London Against Injustice, Kent Against Injustice, Yorkshire and Humberside Against Injustice and West Midlands Against Injustice. South Wales Against Wrongful Conviction remains the only group in Wales to engage in such activities (Poyser, 2012).

The final type of organisation involved in campaigning are groups established by those who have been wrongly accused/convicted of a particular offence. These national support organisations include: the False Allegations Support Organisation (FASO) and People Against False Accusations of Abuse/Support Organisation for Falsely Accused People (PAFAA/SOFAP) (dedicated to those suffering false allegations of abuse); Falsely Accused Carers and Teachers (FACT) (supporting individuals falsely accused of abuse in an occupational setting); Joint Enterprise: Not Guilty by Association (JENGbA) (supporting those wrongly convicted under the joint enterprise law); and The Five Percenters (supporting those wrongly convicted of shaking babies in their care to death) (Poyser, 2012). Some of these organisations have not only helped victims and their families, but also had broader impacts, influencing legislative change. For example, in 2002, FACT provided evidence to a Home Affairs Select Committee that the 'trawling approach' (adopted by police officers to investigate child sexual abuse claims) had caused miscarriages of justice (FACT, no date).

The second and third types of organisation, many of which are run by individuals who have suffered a miscarriage themselves, can offer, in particular, much support to victims and their families. This includes providing recognition, often for the first time since their ordeal began, that something has gone wrong in their cases (Poyser, 2012). Indeed, as a campaigner in the author's research stated: "*just a letter from someone or a visit means the world to people.... In that situation they think the world has turned against them ... they gain spirit from the fact that they know someone believes them*". This research also found that these organisations provide a 'listening ear', open to hearing a family's arguments concerning innocence (again, often for the first time since the conviction occurred).

The regular meetings that they hold provide a platform for families to discuss their cases and to share experiences (Poyser, 2012). Such networking can serve to strengthen a family's resolve to continue fighting the wrongful conviction and to highlight that they are not alone in their fight (PAFAA, no date). Networking also permits families to gain advice from others and to learn new routes through which they might progress their case. For example, families may signpost other families to professionals, such as expert witnesses, who may be able to challenge evidence and others who may provide moral endorsement of a case, having already established a reputation for helping to expose miscarriages (Savage et al, 2007).

Campaigning organisations provide an essential anchorage point and centralised information point from which victims and their families may begin their own campaigning journey (Jenkins, 2014). They offer advice on how to begin challenging a conviction and inform victims of changes in legislation that may impact upon their case. They can also help to set up vigils, marches and petitions, as well as aid families in their attempts to gain a global presence by spreading their message through mainstream media and social media such as Facebook, Twitter and blogging sites (MOJUK, no date).

Journalism

> ... only journalists can investigate the suspected truths that were rejected by the [appellate court] and perhaps firm them up enough to ... persuade a mass readership, and then ... the courts, to accept them. (Walker and Starmer, 1999: 282)

Although the media has contributed to causing miscarriages through, for example, sensationalist/inaccurate coverage of a case prior to, or during, trial (thereby possibly prejudicing a fair trial) (Stephens and Hill, 1999), it has also played a role in helping to overturn wrongful convictions. Chapter Two highlighted how, historically, the involvement of journalists has helped to reveal many miscarriages, both through media campaigns involving storytelling, which have provoked public questioning of a case, and through media investigations, which have uncovered fresh evidence and thereby helped to propel a case back to appeal. Journalists have been involved in helping to reveal wrongful convictions not only for murder (see, eg, Gilmour and Griggs, 1956), but also for lesser offences (see, eg, Brandon and Davies, 1973).

Some journalists have established strong reputations for their involvement in publicising and/or investigating miscarriages, including Paul Foot, Bob Woffinden, Ludovic Kennedy, Eamonn O'Neill, Mark Daly and John Sweeney (Poyser, 2012). The author's research found that publicity can raise the profile of a case, making it something that the authorities cannot ignore. Indeed, as one exoneree outlined: "*Loads of publicity … our case was starting to become a bit more known … people … started realising that there could be a serious miscarriage*". Publicity may also bring a case to the attention of professionals who can lend their advice/expertise (Savage et al, 2007). However, what make the biggest impact in this area are journalistic investigations into alleged miscarriages, as this exoneree outlined:

> They [TV company] investigated the case … that programme was significant because it uncovered … a lot of new evidence. The witnesses admitted that they had been in serious trouble with the police and that they had lied but, more importantly, my co-accused, X, on national TV, said 'I didn't do it … none of us did it'…. I knew we were on our way.

However, the author's research revealed that very few journalists choose to get involved in investigating miscarriages – "*you could probably count on one hand the journalists who are seriously involved*" (TV journalist) – as the work is, according to one journalist, "*emotionally draining and depressing … very slow and labour-intensive*" and, according to another, means that:

> you are not well-liked … mostly the bosses don't like you, the establishment and the powers that be outside don't like you, you are always flirting with libel … it's not nice when the Deputy Chief Constable from X rings up and says they are considering doing you for conspiring to pervert the course of justice … its not nice when you are bugged by Y police as we were in a case, so you go out on a bit out on a limb, once you have done this, you can't really go back into political reporting or whatever.

Media involvement is very much sought after. The investigative journalist has resources, and crucially freedom, to conduct 'full and fearless' investigations into cases, which may result in the discovery of fresh evidence that proves to be crucial at appeal. The latter means that journalists can sometimes act as prisoners' 'court of the last resort' (Hanson, 2011), despite the existence of formal mechanisms to do just this. Journalistic investigations have uncovered fresh evidence in numerous cases, including those where individuals spent decades in prison (see Jessell, 1994). These wrongful convictions may not have been exposed had it not been for media investigations (O'Neill, 2011). The success of this particular informal remedy is undeniable. From 1983 to 2005, for example, the now-defunct investigative TV series 'Rough justice' achieved the quashing of 15 out of 32 convictions examined, and Channel Four's investigative series 'Trial and error' had a success rate of 90% of the convictions investigated later being quashed (Jessell, 1994: 203). This success, according to a journalist in the author's research, comes from "*going out and digging*", that is, 'on-the-ground' investigations involving 'street-level door-knocking and witness-tracking' (O'Neill, 2011: 28) – something that the CCRC has been accused of rarely doing (Woffinden, 2010). The author's research found that it also comes from adopting a 'blank slate' strategy from the start of their enquiries, that is, "*investigating absolutely everything from scratch*" (journalist), rather than investigating only partially within the terms of the 'real possibility test' and general criteria of the appeals system. This may help to explain why journalists are still required to fill an 'investigative gap' in this area. This is of concern as the author's research demonstrated that the establishment of the CCRC led to a major decline in investigative journalism's interest in miscarriages as it was perceived that the journalist's job was done. Indeed, as a solicitor who had worked on miscarriages with the media outlined: "*a whole tranche of investigative journalism in this area disappeared because it was assumed we don't need you any more*". While programmes *dedicated* to this issue ended, pockets of media interest in miscarriages remained and, interestingly, others have more recently reignited with ever-growing criticism of the CCRC because, as one journalist argued, "*the CCRC is perceived to be ... a machinery ... to deal with these things ... my view is ... it doesn't*". Certainly, journalistic involvement in cases is still very much sought after by campaigners.

Importantly, for investigative journalists who *do* remain interested in miscarriages, the Internet has much to offer, particularly in terms of cost-effective methods of sourcing information and people, including international experts who may be able to answer complex questions surrounding a case (Bunz, 2010). It also provides opportunities to draw upon collective knowledge and alternative interpretations of events, and aids journalists in disseminating the results of their investigations to a global audience (McNair, 1998: 141). As a journalist in the author's research revealed, the latter not only allows greater autonomy in terms of what is published; it gets a much bigger audience than "*you can get by putting [it] in a newspaper or on TV ... it's a very powerful medium*".

The power of this medium was demonstrated in late 2014 with the airing of a 12-episode US podcast called 'Serial'. 'Serial' was narrated by a journalist who had investigated an alleged miscarriage in the case of Adnan Syed, who was convicted of murdering his ex-girlfriend in Baltimore in 1999 (Locker, 2016). The podcast captivated the attention of a global audience. Having been downloaded over 60 million times, it was deemed the most popular podcast in the world and to have renewed the public appetite for real-life 'whodunnits' (Brantingham, 2015). The episodes detailed the findings of the journalistic investigation into the case and permitted listeners to scrutinise the evidence and the safety of the conviction (Timm, 2016). Importantly, it also brought forward a crucial new witness who provided a key alibi for Syed and kick-started plans for a new appeal (Brantingham, 2015).

Since the production of 'Serial', many more platforms have become interested in re-examining alleged miscarriages, including Netflix. In December 2015, Netflix released a 10-episode documentary called 'Making a murderer', which chronicled the trial and conviction of Steve Amery for the murder of Teresa Halbach in Wisconsin in 2005. Avery's conviction was shrouded in suspicion because, at the time, he was engaged in suing Manitowoc County for US$36 million after having been wrongly convicted of *another* crime – a brutal rape. His exoneration for this crime came after the real culprit was found and Avery had spent 18 years in prison (*The Guardian*, 2016). There were strong suggestions that Avery had been framed by the police for Halbach's murder, leading two film-makers to spend the next decade following the case. The airing of their findings in a form that left viewers to reach their own conclusions on the evidence presented proved a global hit (Wiseman, 2016). The public responded to the programme's contents by providing new ideas for investigation and setting up petitions calling for Avery's release (Mumford, 2016).

It is indisputable that the networked world *is* now acting as a major source of knowledge, contacts, support and expertise for journalists investigating miscarriages, and that it offers opportunities for collaborations with other investigators worldwide. The Internet can also provide a means of investigative collaboration between citizens and journalists – an area that journalists working in the field of miscarriages have still to fully exploit. However, as we will see, there have certainly been some interesting developments to date.

Citizen journalism

The Internet eliminates the traditional 'top-down' nature of news, permitting a 'bottom-up' role for citizens (Briggs and Burke, 2009). Today, anyone can be a journalist, reporting on daily events and relaying and discussing their experiences via numerous outlets, including 'blogging' and 'tweeting' (Allan, 2006: 166). Describing citizen journalism as 'the spontaneous actions of ordinary people caught up in extraordinary events who felt compelled to adopt the role of news reporter', Greer and McLaughlin (2014: 40) argue that citizen journalists have not just contributed to the news, but sometimes defined it through reporting on events that have been ignored/missed by mainstream journalists. In particular, they highlight the power of the public to publicise a different form of injustice, in particular, the act of a police officer assaulting Ian Tomlinson at London's G20 protests in 2009. Citizen mobile phone footage that contradicted early claims made by the Metropolitan Police regarding the incident was placed on YouTube. This received over 400,000 views and generated intensive blogging (Petrosian, 2014) and a letter-writing campaign to Parliament. It also led to the Tomlinson family setting up a campaign for justice and was key to exposing the truth of what happened at a subsequent inquest into the case, which, in turn, led to the dismissal of the officer involved (Greer and McLaughlin, 2014). Petrosian (2014: 9) argues that, in this case, 'citizen journalism provided the tools and techniques by which a miscarriage of justice was avoided'; however, it might be argued that the footage was actually critical in *revealing* a miscarriage, namely, that Tomlinson's rights as a citizen had been breached.

Greer and McLaughlin's (2014) aforementioned definition of citizen journalism places the citizen in the position of being a 'reactive reporter'. However, more recently, the Internet has provided opportunities for proactive citizen journalism in the form of 'citizen-led investigative journalism' (Allan, 2006). In other genres, citizen-led journalism has demonstrated that being resource-poor has not prevented many major investigations from being conducted (Coronel, 2008: 6). For example, networks such as 'Help Me Investigate' have helped citizens to investigate questions in the public interest (Helpmeinvestigate, no date). These investigations are funded by donations from a virtual campaign group, and report their findings back to that group before divulging them to the world.

Importantly, the Internet and social-networking mediums are also now beginning to be used to muster teams of citizens to investigate aspects of wrongful convictions. For example, the 'WITs justice project online' was set up in South Africa in 2015 by the University of Witswatersrand, Johannesburg. It consists of a criminal justice network aimed at helping marginalised communities to better access justice and focuses upon alleged miscarriages in rural South Africa. It is involved in training local citizens to investigate cases, compile reliable reports and find outlets in which to publish them. These miscarriages would almost certainly go unreported were it not for these citizen investigators (Witsjusticeproject, no date). Citizen-led investigations into miscarriages like these are an informal remedy that we may see more of in the future.[1]

Innocence projects

The Innocence Project was founded in 1992 by legal academics Barry Scheck and Peter Neufeld at Yeshiva University in the US with the aim of exonerating the wrongly convicted through DNA testing. The project brings together paid lawyers and law students to investigate cases where DNA evidence is available to (re-)examine. In the US, to date, over 340 individuals, including 20 death-row inmates, have had their convictions overturned on the basis of the findings of DNA testing by the project (Innocenceproject, no date).

The Innocence Project is the founder of the Innocence Network, a group of Innocence projects dedicated to providing free legal advice and investigative services to the wrongly convicted and working to redress the causes of miscarriages. These projects, established in many universities (predominantly by law and, in some cases, journalism schools), operate in many countries, including Australia, New Zealand, Canada, Italy, Africa, France and, until recently, the UK – an issue returned to shortly (Innocencenetwork, no date). They involve students working on cases where the individual/s involved allege that they have been wrongly convicted,[2] with the aim of aiding them in appealing against their conviction.

In 2004, Bristol University established the Innocence Network UK (INUK), partly in response to concerns that the notion of factual innocence seemed not to be central to the appellate system. From 2004 to 2014, INUK acted as an umbrella organisation for Innocence projects at universities across the UK, facilitating the establishment of, and support to, around 36 of them. These projects provide a free service to victims of alleged miscarriages who have exhausted all other formal options (Eady, 2016). Based within universities, they can access academic experts in policing, pathology and forensic science from internal departments. They also benefit from the input of enthusiastic students, for whom they provide experience of real casework, which is assessed and contributes to their degree award. Such factors mean that Innocence projects offer victims a service that 'No one working under the restrictions of legal-aid funding or the budgetary constraints of the CCRC is likely to' (Eady, 2016). Nevertheless, their success in the UK to date (if measured by referrals from the CCRC to the Court of Appeal) amounts to just three referrals and one conviction quashed (Eady, 2016).[3] This may be partly because UK Innocence projects take on more types of case (ie not just DNA cases) than those in the US. However, Innocence projects also experience broader problems, including the fact that the appellate process is restrictive, meaning that it may be impossible to find new evidence/argument in a case. Importantly, when victims approach Innocence projects, they have usually already 'used up' their best evidence/argument at previous appeals or have had them rejected by the CCRC. Therefore, the cases that UK Innocence projects deal with are usually those in which there are effectively insurmountable barriers to progress (Eady, 2016). Additionally, the casework is complex and time-consuming (Green, 2014).

Some of the problems surrounding the running of Innocence projects resulted in INUK being disbanded in 2015 and the projects affiliated to it effectively becoming individual enterprises, no longer called 'Innocence projects'. An advantage of the disbandment, however, has been that surviving projects have already recognised their new-found freedom to develop their own agendas, for example, choosing to specialise in investigating particular types of miscarriages (Eady, 2016). In addition, there have been efforts to bring the remaining projects together in order to share best practice. In April 2016, a conference held at Cardiff University Law School served as a platform for the coming together of surviving projects. It attempted to discover how different projects worked and managed cases, as well as training needs and the possibility of collaborations (Eady, 2016). Such collaborations are arguably essential for the survival of these projects (Green, 2014).

Charitable projects

In addition to the informal remedies previously mentioned, a number of charitable projects are currently examining alleged miscarriages of justice. One such project is the Centre for Criminal Appeals. A small legal charity set up as a not-for-profit solution to the shortage of investigation/legal representation for appeals, the Centre's stated aims include 'challenging the recurrent and systemic unfairness of the CJS by overturning unsafe convictions and disproportionate sentences' (Centre for Criminal Appeals, no date). In relation to investigating miscarriages, the body uses 'intensive "boots-on-the-ground" investigation to find … crucial missing pieces in a case' (Centre for Criminal Appeals, no date) funded by private donors and grant-makers. Lawyers working for the charity are investigating many cases, including that of the 'Freshwater Five' – five fishermen from the Isle of Wight convicted of attempting to import 255kg of cocaine into the UK in 2010 (Bolton, 2015). The charity raised money through online crowd-funding in order to re-examine this case (Bolton, 2015). However, this is not the only group of lawyers who engage in crowd-funding for justice.

In 2015, a small group of lawyers in London developed an independent funding platform where people could meet as an online community to discuss legal cases, build support for them and share the costs of taking legal action relating to them through crowd-funding. In the face of legal aid cutbacks over more recent years, this group, called 'CrowdJustice', aimed to make it possible for everyone to access the courts (CrowdJustice, no date). One of the first cases shared on CrowdJustice was that of Ameen Jogee, who claimed to have been wrongly convicted of murder in 2012 under the joint enterprise law. His supporters detailed his case to the online community, arguing that the misapplication of this law had contributed to causing his miscarriage and many more. This crowd-fund, entitled 'Change the law on joint enterprise', which tempted the online community to 'be part of a Supreme Court case', succeeded in reaching its target of £10,000 in late 2015. This permitted the campaigning organisation JENGbA to obtain the legal fees required to get Jogee's appeal heard by the Supreme Court. This did not lead to the quashing of Jogee's conviction, but it did lead to legal changes relating to the application of the joint enterprise law (BBC, 2016).

Another project, the Criminal Appeals Lawyers Association (CALA), was formed in 2002 by a group of lawyers wishing to achieve better representation for those seeking to appeal their convictions/sentences (CALA, no date). Its members, who undertake work on a pro bono basis, have made the critical difference to cases where the CCRC has failed to do so. This occurred in the case of Victor Nealon, who was convicted of a brutal attempted rape in 1997 and sentenced to life imprisonment (Mulhall, 2016). He had an appeal dismissed and two applications to the CCRC turned down. A lawyer from CALA persisted in seeking further disclosure of material from the police and, in 2010, was able to organise a DNA test that showed conclusively that someone other than Nealon had deposited DNA on the rape victim. His third application to the CCRC was referred to the Court of Appeal in 2012 and his conviction was quashed (Mulhall, 2016). The effectiveness of this informal remedy was clear as 'There was … no chance … that the CCRC would have persisted in the way that Mr Nealon's solicitor did' (CALA, no date).

A final project to mention is Inside Justice. This not-for-profit charitable unit, a division of *Inside Time*, the national newspaper for prisoners, was established in 2010 by Louise Shorter, one-time producer of the TV series 'Rough justice' (Insidejustice, no date). Its role is to investigate cases where individuals claim to have been convicted of a crime that they did not commit.[4] The unit consists of a panel of experts from forensic science, law, medicine and journalism, who, since its inception, have been asked to investigate close to 1,000 cases (Campbell, 2014). Through engaging in what it calls 'investigative groundwork', the unit's activities involve assessing trial evidence, revisiting witnesses, identifying/commissioning new forensic work and looking at unused material in order to try to discover the new evidence/argument required for an appeal. The unit also provides advice to prisoners and their families, and works with the media to ensure the accurate reporting of miscarriages (Insidejustice, no date).

Family campaigns

While the informal remedies mentioned hitherto may provide support to victims and, in some cases, help to overturn a wrongful conviction, in most cases, it is the prisoner's family who act as the 'nucleus' of the effort and the 'driving force' in the fight against injustice (Savage et al, 2007). Indeed, where informal remedies have succeeded in helping to expose a miscarriage, in most cases, this would have been impossible without the existence of a family campaign. The author's research suggests that the prisoner's family act as the glue, bonding everyone involved in the case together. Their campaigning aim is, first and foremost, to expose their relative's wrongful conviction; however, they may also have longer-term aims, such as persuading the investigating police force to reopen the case after the conviction has been quashed and fighting for changes to policy, practice and/or legislation (Savage et al, 2007).

The discourse of innocence is pivotal to family campaigns, and a key activity that they engage in is to try to exert public pressure on the authorities to engage with this discourse and re-examine a particular case (Jenkins, 2013b). Without the public pressure exerted by family campaigns, some of the most well-known miscarriages, such as the Birmingham Six, may not have been revealed and broader legislative reform may not have occurred (Mansfield, 1993).

Family campaigns usually involve attempts to gain publicity, recognition and support (Morrell, 1999). A critical element in helping family campaigns to achieve success is the formation of links with like-minded individuals who possess expertise and influence, such as lawyers who are known for exerting themselves on behalf of the wrongly convicted (Savage et al, 2007). Support from such entities may also add legitimacy to a family's claims that their loved one has been wrongly convicted, and ultimately establish what Eady (2003: 54) calls a 'chain of fortune', whereby when their involvement becomes known, others may be more inclined to also support the campaign.

Family campaigns engage in a variety of activities to spread their message throughout the public domain, including organising vigils, public protests and petitions. Perhaps the most successful recent family campaign that engaged in these, and many other, activities was the 'Sam Hallam campaign'. Led by Sam's mother, the campaign to reveal his wrongful conviction for murder (in 2005) quickly attracted the attention of Paul May, a veteran miscarriages campaigner, and actor Ray Winston. Soon thereafter, MPs, trade unions, celebrities, singers and religious leaders became involved, thereby demonstrating Eady's (2003) 'chain of fortune' in action. Sam's family engaged in many innovative ventures that gained much media attention. These included: candlelit vigils held outside the offices of the CCRC; a classical music vigil held outside the Ministry of Justice; and Sam's 21st birthday party held outside the gates of the prison wherein he resided (Samhallam, no date). Each event was designed to gain maximum publicity and exert pressure on the CCRC to hasten their re-examination of his conviction. This family's efforts came to fruition when, in 2012, Sam's conviction was quashed (Seabrook, 2016).

While many family campaigns still take to the streets to highlight their relation's plight in the very visual manner of the Hallam campaign, some are increasingly making use of the Internet as a means of disseminating their message (Lomax, 2011). The Internet provides family campaigns with many tools, including: Facebook, Twitter, Tumblr, Youtube and Blogspot. Such tools have helped families to raise awareness of their relative's case, to garner support for their arguments and to sometimes exert public pressure on the authorities to engage in a dialogue with them (Lomax, 2011). Many family campaigns now have an Internet presence, particularly in the form of Facebook pages and individual campaign websites (see, eg, colinnorris.org, no date; justice4kevinnunn. org.uk, no date).

These websites detail aspects of the named prisoner's case, providing chronologies of events leading up to the crime and case documents for visitors to the site to peruse. Almost all have 'tabs' containing newspaper reports on the case, information on campaign events and links to other campaigns. Many websites contain e-petitions that visitors are asked to sign in support of the prisoner (Poyser, forthcoming). Some sites contain requests to trade unions, student unions and other organisations to adopt the case by linking the website banner to their websites. However, as a solicitor in the author's research revealed, while websites, social networking and forums can bring together a 'virtual community' of like-minded individuals, they can also bring misunderstandings, misinformation and attacks from those wishing to undermine the campaign, particularly if the case involves someone claiming to have been wrongly convicted of a highly unpopular offence, wherein "*it really can be a double-edged sword*".

Conclusion

A journalist in the author's research commented that "*Tom Sargant [Secretary of Justice] ... always thought that lay [people] should be involved in reinvestigating miscarriages*". Some would argue that he is right. This chapter has identified and considered informal remedies, involving both lay people *and* professionals, concerned with addressing miscarriages of justice. It has demonstrated that these groups are often vital in supporting victims and their families, and sometimes helping to overturn a wrongful conviction. They may even help to achieve wider reforms in the areas of criminal justice policy/practice/legislation.

It is significant that in the UK (one of the few countries in the world to have a *formal* independent body to review/reinvestigate alleged miscarriages), the call for *informal* remedies to support and help individuals to overturn their convictions is growing so quickly that, as a campaigner in the author's study outlined, "*demand is outstripping supply*". Primarily due to the latter, most of those involved in providing informal remedies are at pains to stress that they can only help individuals claiming to be *innocent* of the crime for which they have been convicted. This is interesting because, as has been stressed throughout this book, even if fresh evidence is uncovered that is strong enough to propel a case back to successful appeal, it does not, of course, mean that the individual concerned is innocent (Naughton, 2007).

As those involved in delivering informal remedies wish to also reduce the causes of miscarriages, it is crucial to also note that technical miscarriages have, at their roots, the same cause/s as those involving innocent individuals. Therefore, while wholly understandable, it is a pity that the commitment of informal remedies to revealing miscarriages is restricted to cases wherein the individual claims to be innocent. The CCRC *is*, of course, prepared to examine *all* claims of wrongful conviction, regardless of whether or not the individual is innocent (CCRC, no date). However, questions surrounding the effectiveness of this formal remedy in getting some cases involving individuals claiming to be innocent past the threshold of 'real possibility' remain. In addition, criticism relating to the degree of 'ground-level' investigative work undertaken continues alongside arguments that desk-bound strategies are insufficient, in many cases, to reveal the fresh evidence required to propel a case back to appeal (Brandon and Davies, 1973). Indeed, as an exoneree in the author's study noted: "*Its what kept me in prison for X years ... because people wouldn't* go out *and ask the questions and find out the truth*". While this situation remains, informal remedies, in terms of both the support they offer to victims and, in some cases, their willingness to undertake investigations into cases, will continue to be required. These things really can sometimes mean the difference between continued incarceration and freedom. Indeed, as a solicitor in the author's research highlighted: "*He would still be inside if it wasn't for what his supporters did on the outside*". Their strength and success in the future, however, is likely to come from broader collaborative efforts and deeper engagement with the networked world (Poyser, forthcoming).

Questions for further consideration

1. Formal remedies exist to recognise and rectify miscarriages of justice. Why, therefore, are many wrongly convicted individuals still dependent upon informal remedies to help them overturn their conviction?

2. What can the 'networked world' offer those campaigning against particular miscarriages of justice?

3. Why do you think the family of the wrongly convicted individual are so important in achieving success in miscarriage of justice campaigns?

Notes

[1] See also UK Supreme Court judgment in *Nunn v Chief Constable of Suffolk Constabulary* [2014] UKSC 37 (Justice, no date), where the importance of such remedies are acknowledged.

[2] The projects only conduct investigations into cases where the appellant claims factual innocence as opposed to those appealing on technical grounds (Jenkins, 2013b).

3   In December 2015, the murder conviction of Dwaine George was overturned as a direct result of the investigation undertaken by students in the Cardiff Innocence Project (Weston, 2016).

4   Indeed, the unit stresses that it will only deal with cases in which the appellant claims factual innocence (Insidejustice, no date).

EIGHT

Conclusion

Angus Nurse

As the early chapters of this book indicate, miscarriages of justice have been an enduring feature of all legal systems since their inception and are inextricably linked to policing discourse. We cannot know how many, or how often, *innocent* individuals are wrongly convicted; however, the notion of the innocent person spending years in prison for a crime that they did not commit remains a powerful narrative that dominates miscarriage of justice discourse (Booker, 2016; Groombridge, 2016; Linehan, 2016). Understandably, campaigners, media commentators and victims of miscarriages focus on the innocent victim wrongly convicted of a crime and serving an unjust punishment. Such manifest unfairness can be symbolic of failings in a system that pits the might of the state against a notionally powerless citizen. The conviction of the innocent creates a powerful narrative about the relentless nature of the criminal justice system (CJS) as being outcomes-driven, with conviction and punishment as the goal. The conviction of the innocent also exemplifies fears about alleged institutional corruption and abuse of state policing powers that potentially result in significant interference with civil liberties. Historically, concerns have been raised about alleged police malpractice, and policing practices are a significant cause of the conviction of the innocent. Yet, as this book illustrates, more commonplace problems of miscarriages are endemic to justice systems in the context of wrongful convictions. In examining this topic, our analysis is concerned with the safety of convictions and the extent to which procedural error raises concerns about the administration of justice. Undoubtedly, some unsafe convictions will involve innocent defendants. However, as previous chapters have shown, the existence of innocence is not a prerequisite for having concerns about miscarriages of justice. This book contends that an understanding of the causes of miscarriages and the manner in which miscarriages continue to take place is integral to developing solutions to the problems caused by wrongful convictions. While it is unlikely that any CJS will ever be infallible, scope exists to learn lessons from miscarriages and to develop mechanisms both to prevent their occurrence and to provide for effective remedies for miscarriage of justice problems. Accordingly, this book's analysis of miscarriages is of direct relevance to contemporary debates in policing and illustrates the manner in which policing and miscarriages of justice remain linked.

Chapter Two of this book provided for a historical overview of key cases. Past experience of wrongful convictions, particularly exposure to miscarriages in murder cases, has arguably had the most influence in prompting criminal justice reform (Brandon and Davies, 1973). Wrongful convictions in such cases not only highlight that the system has likely convicted the innocent, but also reveal that the CJS has failed to convict the guilty. Thus, not only does a killer potentially still walk free, but the CJS has arguably failed in its purpose of uncovering the truth about a crime and meting out the appropriate punishment. In this context, miscarriages of justice represent a failure by the state, both in respect of failing to solve a crime and to convict the guilty party, and in respect of a failure to safeguard society by ensuring the swift and effective administration of justice in order to protect the public. In addition, wrongful convictions have the effect of producing both the direct and indirect victimisation of citizens. Direct impacts are felt by those who are the subject of miscarriages by being the object of investigations that seek to determine their guilt but that may do so by means of guilt-presumptive investigative practices. Ultimately, this can result in an individual being the subject of an abuse of process, where CJS proceedings fail to conform to investigative and criminal procedural rules such that a conviction is considered unsafe due to procedural error. At the extreme end of the scale, rules may be actively subverted such that evidence is manipulated to provide a misleading or even false impression of guilt (see Chapter Three). Indirect impacts of miscarriages of justice are felt by a wider range of citizens, including: the friends and family of the accused; the friends and family of the victim; wider society; and even other CJS professionals whose work is arguably tainted by perceptions of malpractice within the system. Thus, wrongful convictions cast a wide net in terms of the harm they cause, yet they also offer considerable opportunity to learn lessons and to improve criminal justice processes.

Our discussion in previous chapters highlights how historical cases have led to contemporary developments in policing and the administration of justice that are designed to safeguard the rights of suspects and improve the reliability and relevance of evidence used in criminal proceedings. Chapter Two highlights the flaws in cases like the Confait case and the Guildford Four, Maguire Seven and Birmingham Six cases, such that disquiet about miscarriages of justice resulted in the establishment of the Royal Commission on Criminal Justice (RCCJ, 1993). Subsequently, the Criminal Cases Review Commission (CCRC) was established to examine alleged miscarriages and refer them to the Court of Appeal (Hucklesby, 2009), thereby providing a means of independent scrutiny of alleged fault in criminal justice processes. These are important developments in seeking to identify and define the causes of miscarriages of justice and to put in place remedial mechanisms. Yet, they do not mean that miscarriages have been eliminated. The problem of wrongful conviction remains very much a 21st-century problem.

Chapters Three and *Four* identified police investigations as a primary cause of miscarriages of justice. Despite the reforms in criminal justice practices, the additional safeguards provided by regulations such as the Police and Criminal Evidence Act (PACE) (and its associated Codes of Practice) and changes in police interviewing practice, problems undoubtedly continue to exist that cause unsafe convictions. As Chapter Four identifies, miscarriages can be by-products of cognitive phenomena that result in problematic investigative decision-making. This is not to suggest that officers deliberately set out to convict the innocent. Instead, predetermined notions of guilt may create an early investigative theory such that officers commit to a particular case narrative and inadvertently view all evidence through the prism of the accepted view of events (Poyser and Milne, 2015). Arguably, the guilt-presumptive investigation is less a construct of deliberate malpractice than, as Naughton (2011: 41) identifies, a consequence of the pressure placed on investigators to produce results within an adversarial system. In practice, this means directing resources towards constructing a case based primarily on incriminating evidence. Thus, in some cases, investigations focus on that which fits the most expedient narrative and the available evidence is interpreted through the lens of the dominant guilt narrative. Evidence that does not conform to this narrative or that directly challenges it may be discarded or may even be shaped to better fit the preferred narrative (see Chapters Three and Four). In this context, false confessions and errors in investigation become significant issues causing miscarriages, yet they may reflect a genuine belief by investigators that they have identified the correct guilty party. It is broadly acknowledged, at least in England and Wales, that historical police practices failed to safeguard the rights of suspects and arguably allowed investigations to shape evidence to fit a particular narrative. Yet, there is perhaps a failure to recognise that while many issues with investigative practice have improved, such that certain tainted investigative techniques may have been reduced in the UK, problems remain with guilt-presumptive investigation.

Historical investigative problems included such things as oppressive interviews, the abuse of suspects' rights and the fabrication of evidence, such that active corruption was sometimes a feature of investigatory practices where miscarriages were identified (Rozenberg, 1992). Reiner (2000: 168–9) identifies that at the time of the RCCP in the late 1970s, 'there was mounting evidence and complaint about police abuse of powers', while, at the same time, 'the law and order lobby lamented that suspects' rights made the police operate with one hand tied behind their back'. Some 40 years later, the same concerns are not entirely out of place in the context of a post-Human Rights Act world in which some politicians and media commentators claim that human rights concerns hamper effective policing and the smooth running of the CJS (Lester, 2016). Simultaneously, concerns about the ongoing problem of miscarriages of justice remain in place. Reiner (2000: 169) identifies a dual problem: how can the discretion enjoyed by the police be controlled both in a policy sense and in respect of the 'street-level' action of rank-and-file officers, as well as in respect of 'providing channels for complaints about abuse and dissatisfaction'? Contemporary complaint and scrutiny mechanisms do exist in respect of much policing activity, for example, by way of complaints to the Independent Office for Police Conduct (formerly the Independent Police Complaints Commission, IPCC) and human rights challenges through the courts. However, the reality for many victims of miscarriages is that formal remedies for victimisation tend only to bite once a wrongful conviction has taken place.

Chapter Five illustrated the victimisation inherent in miscarriages of justice, which is arguably twofold. First, those who are the subjects of miscarriages suffer direct victimisation in the context of having errors in the criminal justice process directly impact upon their fair trial rights and often their liberty. Second, the impacts of miscarriages are felt by a range of secondary victims and the general public. In one sense, whether the victim is guilty or innocent is irrelevant.

As Chapter Three indicated, Article 6 of the European Convention on Human Rights (ECHR) requires that a trial should be a fair process conducted before an independent and impartial tribunal. The obligations under Article 6 are not limited to a presumption of innocence or the requirement for the state to provide legal representation (where a defendant cannot afford the means to secure such representation). Article 6 also lays down safeguards in respect of the right to effective counsel and to be able to examine witnesses and evidence. Fairness thus dictates compliance with formal criminal procedure rules designed to protect the integrity of the trial process and to safeguard the rights of defendants when faced with the might of the state criminal justice apparatus. Practices that prevent the defendant from receiving a fair trial, which may include the existence of evidential irregularities such that a defendant may be unable to effectively defend themselves, may be problematic. Non-disclosure of evidence, for example, is identified as a factor in contemporary miscarriages, where non-disclosure or failings in disclosure impact negatively on the defendant's ability to mount a robust and effective defence. Article 6, therefore, links to a number of issues raised throughout this book, particularly in respect of investigative practices and procedural issues that may give rise to wrongful convictions.

Secondary victimisation occurs in respect of the harm that miscarriages of justice cause to family members and wider society. Arguably, victimisation is worse for the innocent individual who is convicted for a crime that they did not commit than for the guilty individual convicted via a flawed process. However, both are victims of CJS failures, something that the state is arguably slow to realise. Indeed, it could be argued that by predicating the payment of compensation on notions of *proven* innocence (Zander, 2013; Campbell, 2015), the state is tightly constraining its recognition of victimisation to selected issues. In *Mullen* [2002] EWHC 230, Lord Bingham commented that the Court of Appeal had concluded that Mr Mullen was the victim of a gross abuse of executive power. The Court also held that the British authorities had acted in breach of international law and had been guilty of 'a blatant and extremely serious failure to adhere to the rule of law with regard to the production of a defendant for prosecution in the English courts' (para 7). Yet, the House of Lords[1] restored the Court's original ruling, with Lord Steyn stating that only someone who was *clearly innocent* was entitled to compensation. While Lord Bingham and the other Law Lords acknowledged that the statutory miscarriage of justice compensation scheme also provided for compensation in cases where there had been a serious failure in the trial process, this did not apply in the Mullen case. English case law has now clarified that compensation will only be granted to the innocent but the reality of miscarriage of justice victimisation is such that actually *proving* innocence is often problematic unless somebody else is convicted of the crime. Irrespective of this, those convicted of a crime via an abuse of process or accidental procedural error are still victims of a miscarriage, irrespective of the state's (un)willingness to acknowledge this fact. Arguably, where the state makes an error, some form of redress is required, and it remains a problematic area of miscarriage of justice discourse and policy that remedies arguably fail to address the real harm caused by miscarriages.

Research into miscarriages of justice has identified the problems with appellate and review mechanisms, as set out in earlier chapters of this book. The question arises as to how should miscarriages and their associated harms and injustices be remedied? *Chapter Seven* identified that informal remedies are required because formal remedies often prove inadequate. Both the CCRC and the Court of Appeal might be seen as failing because they are reluctant to involve themselves in innocence claims (Naughton, 2011). Instead, both bodies have arguably prioritised procedural and technical grounds of appeal over direct consideration of factual innocence (McCartney and Roberts, 2012). The Court of Appeal, in particular, has been criticised for an apparent unwillingness to consider whether juries have simply got it wrong. Yet, Chapter Seven also identified that informal remedies that identify fresh evidence in a case remain bound by the jurisdictional and procedural practices of the Court of Appeal and the CCRC. Thus, an informal remedy, such as a campaign or journalistic inquiry, may well identify a flaw in a conviction such that there are grounds for making an application to the CCRC. Yet, as *Chapter Six* identified, the CCRC remains bound by the 'real possibility' test contained in the Criminal Appeal Act 1995. This test, set out in legislation, arguably limits the extent to which the CCRC can reasonably be expected to refer a case to the Court of Appeal, particularly where there are doubts that doing so will result in the appellate court actively considering the case. How the CCRC should apply the 'real possibility' test risks being an area of conflict between the CCRC and its critics.

As Chapter Six outlined, the CCRC has been accused of being too cautious in its referrals to the Court of Appeal and of failing to directly engage with factual innocence concerns. The Court of Appeal's jurisprudence arguably also restricts the CCRC in its determinations by dictating the likely success or otherwise of referrals, thus setting a threshold for CCRC decisions. There is, of course, an argument that the CCRC could be bolder in its applications to the Court of Appeal and that its unique position could provide valuable information on lessons for CJS processes and preventing miscarriages. We explored these issues in Chapter Six and suggested that there is scope to develop the role of the CCRC so that its casework and investigative findings add value to the miscarriage of justice landscape beyond that of individual case outcomes. Where appellate mechanisms or the CCRC fail to provide for a remedy, then informal remedies become vital to addressing miscarriage issues and providing support to victims. However, as Chapter Seven identified, the call for informal remedies is growing such that demand is outstripping supply.

Undoubtedly, there is recognition that historical policing practices were a significant factor in the existence of miscarriages of justice. Accordingly, there have been significant changes in the law relating to investigative practice, police accountability and the clarification of the law concerning appeals for miscarriages. There have also been considerable developments in police training, including evidence-based practice. The creation of the CCRC is an important step forward in providing a route through which miscarriage of justice cases might be pursued. Yet, it falls short of being the arbiter of innocence that was arguably envisaged when it was set up, even though its casework (where it ultimately results in convictions being quashed) has the effect of nullifying wrongful convictions. In some respects, this book identifies that the British CJS remains at a crossroads in respect of how it deals with miscarriages. The perceived widespread malpractice of the past has, to some extent, been addressed through legislative, procedural and regulatory reform. Yet, wrongful convictions continue to occur and concerns remain about the efficacy of appellate and redress mechanisms. The CJS should arguably correct and police itself, and be sufficiently robust that both procedural errors and factual innocence are caught either during the trial process or via appellate or CCRC review. Particularly where evidence exists to cast doubt on whether the right person has been convicted, justice systems should not only provide for a declaration concerning the unsafe nature of convictions, but also address the harm caused by miscarriages. In this respect, the continued existence of miscarriages and the limited success of remedies, as identified during this book, suggest that our adversarial system cannot be said to protect the innocent, but neither can it be said to have in place truly appropriate mechanisms to deal with miscarriages of justice problems when they have occurred.

In writing this book, we have sought to provide an overview of contemporary miscarriage of justice issues and identify some key areas for discussion. Our analysis does not claim to be definitive, although we have explored selected issues in some detail and have examined changes in both law and procedure. We have also sought to identify the extent to which miscarriages of justice are central issues in policing discourse and to consider the extent to which they provide lessons in respect of both contemporary policing practice and the impact of policing on citizens and wider society. Policing lies at the heart of miscarriages of justice, both directly and indirectly. From a suspect's first engagement with the police as investigators, through to disclosure of evidence uncovered during an investigation and presentation of evidence at trial, policing and prosecution practice arising from the investigative process offers scope to cause or prevent a miscarriage of justice from occurring. Miscarriage of justice discourse and associated areas of policing, criminal law and human rights law are fast-moving areas and we anticipate having to re-examine some areas of our analysis in light of developments in the courts, in policy and in policing and prosecutions practice. We look forward to doing so.

Note

[1]   The case pre-dates the creation of the Supreme Court; thus, at the time, the House of Lords was the highest appellate court (except in Scotland).

References

Acker, J. (2012) 'The flipside injustice of wrongful convictions: when the guilty go free', *Albany Law Review*, 76: 1629–712.

ACPO (Association of Chief Police Officers) (2006) *Murder investigation manual*, London: National Centre for Policing Excellence.

ACPO (2012) *Practical advice on critical incident management* (2nd edn), Wyboston: NPIA.

Addley, E. (2016) '"I want to be a voice for the voiceless," says nun left in limbo over sex abuse allegations', *The Guardian*, 2 April. Available at: http://www.theguardian.com/society/2016/apr/02/i-want-to-be-a-voice-for-the-voiceless-says-helen-house-nun-left-in-limbo-over-sex-abuse-allegations (accessed 14 July 2016).

Allan, S. (2006) *Online news: Journalism and the Internet*, Oxford: OUP.

Allen, K. (2016) 'UK Supreme Court overturns "joint enterprise" interpretation', *Politics and Policy*, 18 February. Available at: http://www.ft.com/cms/s/0/cf6f7dfa-d630-11e5-8887-98e7feb46f27.html#axzz41ky7PAWF (accessed 23 May 2016).

Allison, E. (2015) 'Newspaper's prison correspondent says more innocent people are being jailed', *Prison Watch UK*. Available at: https://prisonwatchuk.com/tag/jail/ (accessed 26 November 2015).

Ambler, C. and Milne, R. (2006) 'Call handling centres: an evidential opportunity or threat?', paper presented at the Second International investigative Interviewing Conference, University of Portsmouth, UK.

Ask, K. and Granhag, P.A. (2005) 'Motivational sources of confirmation bias in criminal investigations: the need for cognitive closure', *Journal of Investigative Psychology and Offender Profiling*, 2: 43–63.

Ask, K., Rebellius, A. and Granhag, P.A. (2008) 'The elasticity of criminal evidence: a moderator of investigator bias', *Applied Cognitive Psychology*, 22: 1245–59.

Ayling, C.J. (1984) 'Corroborating confessions: an empirical analysis of legal safeguards against false confessions', *Wisconsin Law Review*, 4: 1121–204.

Baksi, C. (2014) 'Cuts forcing guilty pleas, leading lawyer warns', *Law Society Gazette*, 10 February. Available at: https://www.lawgazette.co.uk/law/most-victims-unable-to-access-legal-aid/analysis/letters/gulf-in-access-to-justice/practice/cuts-forcing-guilty-pleas-leading-lawyer-warns/5039818.article (accessed 31 July 2017).

Baldwin, J. (1992) *Video-taping police interviews with suspects: A national evaluation*, Police Research Series Paper 1, London: HMSO.

Baldwin, J. (1993) 'Police interviewing techniques. Establishing truth or proof?', *British Journal of Criminology*, 33: 325–52.

Baldwin, J. and McConville, M. (1979) *Jury trials*, London: Clarendon.

Baldwin, J. and McConville, M. (1981) *Confessions in Crown Court trials*, Research Study No 5, Royal Commission on Criminal Procedure, Cmnd 8092, London: HMSO.

Bartholemew, E. (2015) 'Miscarriage of justice victim, Sam Hallam denied compensation', *Hackney Gazette*, 10 June. Available at: http://www.hackneygazette.co.uk/news/crime-court/miscarriage_of_justice_victim_sam_hallam_denied_compensation_1_4106522 (accessed 12 July 2016).

Batt, J. (2004) *Stolen innocence: The Sally Clark story – a mother's fight for justice*, London: Ebury Press.

Baumgartner, F.R., Grigg, A., Ramirez, R., Rose, K.J. and Lucy, J.S. (2014) 'The mayhem of wrongful liberty: documenting the crimes of true perpetrators in cases of wrongful incarceration', paper presented at the Innocence Network Annual Conference, Portland, Oregon, US, 11–12 April.

BBC (2012) 'Family killer Jeremy Bamber fails in appeal bid', 26 April. Available at: http://www.bbc.co.uk/news/uk-england-essex-17851314 (accessed 12 June 2015).

BBC (2016) 'Ameen Jogee to be retried after successful joint enterprise appeal', 8 April. Available at: http://www.bbc.co.uk/news/uk-england-leicestershire-35996076 (accessed 9 April 2016).

Bearchell, J. (2010) 'UK police interviews with suspects: a short modern history', in J. Adler and J. Gray (eds) *Forensic psychology: Concepts, debates and practice*, Cullompton: Willan, pp 73–88.

Bedau, H.A. and Radelet, M.L. (1987) 'Miscarriages of justice in potentially capital cases', *Stanford Law Review*, 40: 21–179.

Belloni, F. and Hodgson, J. (2000) *Criminal injustice: An evaluation of the criminal justice process in Britain*, London: Palgrave Macmillan.

Bennetto, J. (2003) 'Convicted after 15 years: the prostitute's killer who watched three men go to jail for his crime', *The Independent*, 4 July. Available at: http://www.independent.co.uk/news/uk/crime/convicted-after-15-years-the-prostitutes-killer-who-watched-three-men-go-to-jail-for-his-crime-94860.html (accessed 20 December 2016).

Bernhard, A. (1999) 'When justice fails: indemnification for unjust conviction', University of Chicago Law School, Roundtable, 6: 73–122.

Birch, D. (2014) 'Did she kill him? Review: a Victorian scandal of sex and poisoning', *The Guardian*, 25 February. Available at: https://www.theguardian.com/books/2014/feb/25/did-she-kill-him-kate-colquhoun-review (accessed 21 May 2016).

Blackstone, W. (1858) *Commentaries on the laws of England* (9th edn), Oxford: Clarendon Press.

Block, B.P. and Hostettler, J. (1997) *Hanging in the balance: A history of the abolition of capital punishment in Britain*, London: Waterside Press.

BMJ (*British Medical Journal*) (2000) 'Conviction by mathematical error? Doctors and lawyers should get probability theory right'. Available at: http://www.bmj.com/content/320/7226/2 (accessed 24 June 2016).

Bolton, E. (2015) 'How long is it acceptable for a person to stay in prison for a crime they didn't commit?', *The Justice Gap*, 27 March. Available at: http://thejusticegap.com/2015/03/how-long-is-it-acceptable-a-person-stay-in-prison-for-a-crime-they-didnt-commit/ (accessed 24 June 2015).

Booker, C. (2016) 'After "Making a Murderer" miscarriages of justice are in the spotlight', *Huffington Post*. Available at: http://www.huffingtonpost.co.uk/simon-booker/making-a-murderer_b_9165560.html (accessed 4 February 2017).

Borchard, E.M. (1932) *Convicting the innocent: Sixty-five actual errors of criminal justice*, Garden City, NY: Doubleday.

Bowcott, O. (2014) 'Police rebuked over handling of interviews with child sex abuse victims', *The Guardian*, 18 December. Available at: https://www.theguardian.com/uk-news/2014/dec/18/review-child-sex-abuse-victims-police-hmcpsi-hmic (accessed 24 August 2016).

Bowcott, O. (2015) 'Victims of crime let down by criminal justice system, report finds', *The Guardian*, 27 January. Available at: https://www.theguardian.com/uk-news/2015/jan/27/victims-crime-let-down-criminal-justice-newlove (accessed 12 August 2015).

Bowcott, O. (2016) 'Review mandatory life sentences for murder, says joint enterprise report', *The Guardian*, 5 July. Available at: https://www.theguardian.com/law/2016/jul/05/review-mandatory-life-sentences-for-says-joint-enterprise-report (accessed 3 December 2016).

Brandon, R. and Davies, C. (1973) *Wrongful imprisonment: Mistaken convictions and their consequences*, London: Allen and Unwin.

Brantingham, W. (2015) 'How "Serial" shined a light on our troubled justice system', *PBS Newshow*, 8 June. Available at: http://www.pbs.org/newshour/bb/serial-shined-light-troubled-justice-system/ (accessed 12 May 2016).

Briggs, A. and Burke, P. (2009) *Social history of the media: From Gutenberg to the Internet*, London: Polity Press.

Brookman, F. and Innes, M. (2013) 'The problem of success: what is a "good" homicide investigation?', *Policing and Society*, 23(3): 292–310.

Bull, R. (1999) 'Police investigative interviewing', in A. Memon and R. Bull (eds) *Handbook of the psychology of interviewing*, Chichester: Wiley, pp 279–92.

Bunz, M. (2010) 'How investigative reporting makes use of the Internet', *The Guardian*, 23 March. Available at: http://www.guardian.co.uk/media/pda/2010/mar/22/investigative-journalism-layer-reporting (accessed 25 March 2010).

Burrell, I. (1999) 'West Midlands Serious Crime Squad: police unit to blame for "dozens more injustices"', *The Independent*, 1 November. Available at: http://www.independent.co.uk/news/west-midlands-serious-crime-squad-police-unit-to-blame-for-dozens-more-injustices-1120219.html (accessed 12 July 2017).

Burtt, E. (forthcoming) 'Inside: claiming wrongful conviction in prison', unpublished PhD thesis, University of Oxford Centre for Criminology, UK.

CALA (Criminal Appeals Lawyers Association) (no date) 'Appendix 3 statement of CALA'. Available at: http://2bquk8cdew6192tsu41lay8t.wpengine.netdna-cdn.com/wp-content/uploads/2014/12/Statement-of-Criminal-Appeal-Lawyers-Association.pdf (accessed 14 July 2016).

Callan, K. (1998) *Kevin Callan's story*, London: Time Warner Paperbacks.

Campbell, D. (2012) 'The Cardiff Three: the long wait for justice', *The Guardian*, 17 September. Available at: http://www.guardian.co.uk/uk/2012/sep/17/cardiff-three-five-wait-justice (accessed 20 August 2016).

Campbell, D. (2014) 'Inside justice puts list of miscarriage cases and TV programme archive online', *The Guardian*, 16 June. Available at: https://www.theguardian.com/uk-news/2014/jun/16/inside-justice-miscarriage-list-online-archive-films (accessed 24 June 2016).

Campbell, D. (2015) 'Why is Britain refusing to compensate victims of miscarriage of justice?', *The Guardian*, 23 February. Available at: https://www.theguardian.com/commentisfree/2015/feb/23/britain-refusing-compensate-victims-miscarriage-justice (accessed 16 December 2016).

Campbell, K. and Denov, M. (2004) 'The burden of innocence: coping with a wrongful imprisonment', *Canadian Journal of Criminology and Criminal Justice*, 46: 139–64.

Cannings, A. (2006) *Against all odds: A mother's fight to prove her innocence*, London: Time Warner Books.

Cathcart, B. (2004) 'The strange case of Adolf Beck', *The Independent*, 16 October. Available at: http://www.independent.co.uk/news/uk/crime/the-strange-case-of-adolf-beck-535209.html (accessed 12 June 2016).

CCRC (Criminal Cases Review Commission) (no date) 'What we do'. Accessed 12 August 2016 (but no longer available) at: http://ccrc.wpengine.com/about-us/what-we-do/).

CCRC (2012) 'Case library'. Available at: http://www.justice.gov.uk/about/criminal-cases-review-commission/case-library (accessed 20 June 2012).

CCRC (2015) 'Annual report and accounts 2014/15'. Available at: http://www.ccrc.gov.uk/wp-content/uploads/2015/07/CCRC-Annual-Report-and-Accounts-2014-15.pdf (accessed 12 August 2016).

CCRC (2017a) 'Case statistics'. Available at: https://ccrc.gov.uk/case-statistics/ (accessed 17 August 2017).

CCRC (2017b) 'Press releases'. Available at: http://www.ccrc.gov.uk/press-releases/ (accessed 17 February 2017).

Centre for Criminal Appeals (no date) 'Home page'. Available at: http://www.criminalappeals.org.uk/ (accessed 17 August 2016).

Centrex (2005a) *Professionalising police investigation programme*, London: National Centre for Policing Excellence.

Centrex (2005b) *Core investigative doctrine*, London: National Centre for Policing Excellence.

Chambliss, W.J. (1989) 'State organised crime. The American Society of Criminology, presidential address', *Criminology*, 27(2): 183–208.

Children's Commissioner (2015) *Protecting children from harm: A critical assessment of child sexual abuse in the family network in England and priorities for action. Summary: November 2015*, London: Children's Commissioner for England. Accessed 28 July 2016 (but no longer available) at: https://www.childrenscommissioner.gov.uk/sites/default/files/publications/Protecting%20children%20from%20harm%20-%20executive%20summary_0.pdf

Chinn, J. and Ratcliff, A. (2009) '"I was put out the door with nothing" – addressing the needs of the exonerated under a refugee model', *California Western Law Review*, 45(2): 405–44.

Christian, P. (2013) 'Sherlock Holmes and the curious case of Welwyn Garden City man George Edalji', *Welwyn Hatfield Times*, 17 June. Available at: http://www.whtimes.co.uk/news/sherlock_holmes_and_the_curious_case_of_welwyn_garden_city_man_george_edalji_1_2232724 (accessed 29 May 2016).

Clarke, C. and Milne, R. (2001) *National evaluation of the PEACE investigative interviewing course*, London: Home Office.

Clarke, C. and Milne, R. (2016) 'Interviewing suspects in England and Wales: a national evaluation of PEACE interviewing one decade later', in D. Walsh, G. Oxburgh, A. Redlich and T. Mykleburst (eds) *International developments and practices in investigative interviewing and interrogation, vol 2. Suspects*, London: Routledge, pp 21–44.

Clarke, C., Milne, R. and Bull, R. (forthcoming) 'Real life interview with victims and witnesses of crime: crime seriousness', *Psychology, Public Policy and Law*.

Clemmer, D. (1958) *The prison community*, New York, NY: Rinehart.

Clifford, B.R. and Bull, R. (1978) *The psychology of person identification*, London: Routledge.

Clow, K.A., Leach, A.M. and Riccardelli, R. (2012) 'Life after wrongful conviction', in B. Cutler (ed) *Conviction of the innocent: Lessons from psychological research*, Washington, DC: American Psychological Association, pp 327–41.

Coates, T. (2001) *The strange case of Adolf Beck*, London: Stationery Office.

Cole, S. (2009) 'Cultural consequences of miscarriages of justice', *Behavioural Sciences and the Law*, 27: 431–49.

Colinnorris.org (no date) 'Home page'. Available at: http://colinnorris.org/index.html (accessed 17 August 2015).

College of Policing (2017) 'Working with suspects'. Available at: https://www.app.college.police.uk/app-content/investigations/working-with-suspects/ (accessed 1 August 2017).

Colquhoun, K. (2014) 'Life story: addiction, adultery and a very Victorian scandal', *The Daily Mail*, 16 February. Available at: http://www.dailymail.co.uk/home/you/article-2557794/Addiction-adultery-Victorian-scandal.html (accessed 27 April 2016).

Colquhoun, K. (2015) *Did she kill him? A Victorian tale of deception, adultery & arsenic*, London: Little Brown.

Conlon, G. (1994) *Proved innocent: The story of Gerry Conlon of the Guildford Four*, London: Penguin.

Connors, E., Lundregan, T., Miller, N. and McEwen, T. (1996) *Convicted by juries, exonerated by science: Case studies in the use of DNA evidence to establish innocence after trial*, Rockville: National Institute of Justice.

Conway, M.A. (2008) *Guidelines on memory and the law: Recommendations from the scientific study of human memory*, Leicester: British Psychological Society.

Coronel, S. (2008) *The media as watchdog*, Harvard: Harvard University Press.

CPTU (Central Planning and Training Unit) (1992a) *The interviewer's rule book*, London: Home Office.

CPTU (1992b) *A guide to interviewing*, London: Home Office.

CrowdJustice (no date) 'Home page'. Available at: https://www.crowdjustice.co.uk/ (accessed 28 June 2016).

Cutler, B. (2012) *Convictions of the innocent: Lessons from psychological research*, Washington, DC: American Psychological Association.

Dando, C., Wilcock, R. and Milne, R. (2008a) 'The cognitive interview: inexperienced police officers' perceptions of their witness/victim interviewing practices', *Legal and Criminological Psychology*, 13: 59–70.

Dando, C., Wilcock, R. and Milne R. (2008b) 'The cognitive interview: the efficacy of a modified mental reinstatement of context procedure for frontline police investigators', *Applied Cognitive Psychology*, 23: 138–47.

Death Penalty Information Centre (2016) *Death Penalty Factsheet*, Washington, DC: DPIC. Available at: http://www.deathpenaltyinfo.org/documents/FactSheet.pdf (accessed 23 December 2016).

Devlin, P., Lord (1976) *Report to the Secretary of State for the Home Department of the Departmental Committee on Evidence of Identification in Criminal Cases*, 26 April, London: HMSO.

Dodd, V. (2016a) 'Operation Midland has not found enough evidence to charge any suspects', *The Guardian*, 14 February. Available at: http://www.theguardian.com/uk-news/2016/feb/14/operation-midland-nick-establishment-sexual-abuse (accessed 24 June 2016).

Dodd, V. (2016b) 'Scotland Yard launches inquiry into its handling of abuse allegations', *The Guardian*, 10 February. Available at: http://www.theguardian.com/uk-news/2016/feb/10/scotland-yard-inquiry-handling-of-abuse-allegations-brittan-bramall (accessed 24 August 2016).

Dodd, V. (2017) 'Forensic science cuts pose risk to justice, regulator warns', *The Guardian*, 6 January. Available at: https://www.theguardian.com/science/2017/jan/06/forensic-science-cuts-pose-risk-justice-regulator-warns (accessed 25 April 2017).

Doyle, J.M. (2013) 'An etiology of wrongful convictions', in M. Zalman and J. Carrano (eds) *Wrongful conviction and criminal justice reform: Making justice*, New York, NY: Routledge, pp 56–72.

Drizin, S.A. and Leo, R.A. (2004) 'The problem of false confessions in the post-DNA world', *North Carolina Law Review*, 82: 891–1007.

Dugan, E. (2015) 'Crippling court costs force poverty-stricken people to "plead guilty to crimes they didn't commit"', *The Independent*, 21 August. Available at: http://www.independent.co.uk/news/uk/crime/crippling-court-costs-force-poverty-stricken-people-to-plead-guilty-to-crimes-they-didnt-commit-10466451.html (accessed 31 July 2017).

Durkheim, E. (1897) *Suicide: A study in sociology*, New York, NY: The Free Press.

Dyer, C. (2003) 'My sister Ruth', *The Guardian*, 12 September. Available at: http://www.theguardian.com/uk/2003/sep/12/ukcrime.claredyer (accessed 12 May 2016).

Eady, D. (2003) 'A study of 12 miscarriages of justice in Wales', unpublished master's dissertation, Cardiff University, UK.

Eady, D. (2016) 'Lecture on informal remedies against miscarriages of justice', BA Criminology, miscarriages of justice module, Nottingham Trent University, UK, 12 March.

Eady, D. and Price, J. (2013) 'Defending in the realm of denial and fallibility', in J. Robins (ed) *No defence: Lawyers and miscarriages of justice*, London: The Justice Gap, pp 22–7.

Eddiegilfoyle (no date) 'Home page'. Available at: http://eddiegilfoyle.co.uk/ (accessed 20 June 2014).

Eddleston, J. (2009) *Miscarriages of justice: Famous London cases*, Barnsley: Wharncliffe Books.

Eddleston, J. (2012a) *Miscarriages of justice: Famous London cases*, Barnsley: Wharncliff Books.

Eddleston, J. (2012b) *Blind justice: Miscarriages of justice in 20th century Britain*, Santa Barbara, CA: ABC-CLIO.

Edmond, G. (2002) 'Constructing miscarriages of justice: misunderstanding scientific evidence in high profile criminal appeals', *Oxford Journal of Legal Studies*, 22(1): 53–89.

Egbuonu, E. (2015) 'Joint enterprise law criminalises young, black men. It urgently needs reform', *The Guardian*, 22 September. Available at: https://www.theguardian.com/society/2015/sep/22/joint-enterprise-criminalise-young-people-reform-guilt-association (accessed 22 October 2015).

Etter, B. (2012) 'The contribution of "corruption" to miscarriage of justice cases'. Available at: http://www.corruptionprevention.net/assets/Resources/Barbara-Etter-Paper.pdf (accessed 22 December 2016).

Evans, K. (2012) 'Hallam's case will send shockwaves through criminal justice system', *The Guardian*, 17 May. Available at: http://www.guardian.co.uk/law/2012/may/17/sam-hallam-shockwaves-criminal-justice-system (accessed 16 December 2016).

Evans, M. (2012) 'Sian O'Callaghan killer escaped justice for second murder after police blunder', *The Telegraph*, 19 October. Available at: http://www.telegraph.co.uk/news/uknews/crime/9619952/Sian-OCallaghan-killer-escapes-justice-for-second-murder-after-police-blunder.html (accessed 22 August 2016).

Evans, R. (1993) *The conduct of police interviews with juveniles*, Royal Commission on Criminal Justice, Research Report No. 8, London: HMSO.

Evans, R. (2014) 'Drax protesters' convictions quashed over withheld evidence of police spy', *The Guardian*, 21 January. Available at: https://www.theguardian.com/uk-news/2014/jan/21/drax-protesters-convictions-quashed-police-spy-mark-kennedy (accessed 12 August 2016).

Ewick, P. (2009) 'The scale of injustice', in C.J. Ogletree and A. Sarat (eds) *When law fails: Making sense of miscarriages of justice*, New York, NY: NYP, pp 303–28.

FACT (Falsely Accused Carers and Teachers) (no date) 'Advisory group to FACT'. Available at: http://www.factuk.org/wp-content/uploads/2015/01/FACT-Advisory-Group-Issue-2_11-03-15.pdf (accessed 22 June 2016).

Fahsing, I. (2016) *The making of an expert detective: Thinking and deciding in criminal investigations*, Gothenburg: University of Gothenburg.

Findlay, K. (2012) 'Adversarial inquisitions: rethinking the search for the truth', *New York Law School Law Review*, 56(3): 911–41.

Findlay, M. (2008) 'Juror comprehension and the hard case – making forensic evidence simpler', *International Journal of Law Crime and Justice*, 36(1): 15–53.

Findley, K.A. (2012) 'Tunnel vision', in B.L. Cutler (ed) *Conviction of the innocent: Lessons from psychological research*, Washington, DC: American Psychological Association, pp 303–23.

Findley, K.A. and O'Brien, B. (2014) 'Psychological perspectives: cognition and decision-making', in A. Redlich, J.R. Acker, R.J. Norris and C.L. Bonventre (eds) *Examining wrongful convictions: Stepping back, moving forward*, Carolina: Carolina Academic Press, pp 35–53.

Fisher, R. and Geiselman, R. (1992) *Memory-enhancing techniques for investigative interviewing: The cognitive interview*, Springfield, IL: Thomas.

Fisher, R., Milne, R. and Bull, R. (2011) 'Interviewing cooperative witnesses', *Current Directions in Psychological Science*, 20(1): 16–19.

Fleming, P. (2000) *Sudden unexpected deaths in infancy: The CESDI-SUDI studies, 1993–1996*, London: The Stationery Office.

Forst, B. (2004) *Errors of justice: Nature, sources, and remedies*, Cambridge: Cambridge University Press.

Forst, B. (2013) 'Wrongful convictions in a world of miscarriages of justice', in C.R. Huff and M. Killias (eds) *Wrongful conviction and miscarriages of justice: Causes and remedies in North American and European criminal justice systems*, London: Routledge, pp 15–43.

Frank, J. and Frank, B. (1957) *Not guilty*, New York, NY: Doubleday.

Frederichs, D. (2004) *Trusted criminals: White-collar crime in contemporary society*, Belmont, CA: Wadsworth.

Gabbert, F., Hope, L. and Fisher, R.P. (2009) 'Protecting eyewitness evidence: examining the efficacy of a self-administered interview tool', *Law and Human Behaviour*, 33: 298–307.

Gabbert, F., Hope, L., Carter, E., Boon, R. and Fisher, R.P. (2016) 'The role of initial witness accounts within the investigative process', in G. Oxburgh, T. Myklebust, T. Grant and R. Milne (eds) *Communication in investigative and legal contexts: Integrated approaches from forensic psychology, linguistics and law enforcement*, Chichester: Wiley, pp 107–32.

George, M. (2015) 'Why blame the CCRC? Its the Court of Appeal that needs to change', *The Justice Gap*, 19 April. Available at: http://thejusticegap.com/2015/04/blaming-the-ccrc-its-the-attitude-and-culture-of-the-court-of-appeal-that-needs-to-change-not-the-ccrc/ (accessed 27 February 2017).

Giddens, A. (1984) *The constitution of society*, Cambridge: Polity Press.

Gill, P. (2014) *Misleading DNA evidence: Reasons for miscarriages of justice*, London: Academic Press.

Gill, P. (2016) 'Analysis and implications of the miscarriages of justice of Amanda Knox and Raffaele Sollecito', *Forensic Science International: Genetics*, 23: 9–18.

Gilmour, I. and Griggs, J. (1956) *Timothy Evans: An appeal to reform*, London: Spectator.

Goffman, E. (1963) *Stigma: Notes on the management of spoiled identity*, Upper Saddle River, NJ: Prentice Hall.

Gould, J.B. and Leo, R.A. (2010) 'One hundred years later: wrongful convictions after a century of research', *Journal of Criminal Law and Criminology*, 100(3): 825–68.

Green, A. (2014) 'UK innocence projects: a bright future', *The Justice Gap*, 21 August. Available at: http://thejusticegap.com/2014/08/uk-innocence-projects-bright-future/ (accessed 12 August 2015).

Green, A. and McGourlay, C. (2015) 'The wolf packs in our midst and other products of criminal joint enterprise prosecutions', *Journal of Criminal Law*, 79(4): 234–80.

Greer, C. and McLaughlin, E. (2014) 'Righting wrongs: citizen journalism and miscarriages of justice', in S. Allan and E. Thorsen (eds) *Citizen journalism: Global perspectives, volume 2*, London: Peter Lang, pp 39–50.

Greer, S. (1994) 'Miscarriages of criminal justice reconsidered', *The Modern Law Review*, 57(1): 58–74.

Griffiths, A. and Milne, R. (2006) 'Will it all end in tiers? Police interviews with suspects in Britain', in T. Williamson (ed) *Investigative interviewing: Rights, research and regulation*, Cullumpton: Willan, pp 167–89.

Griffiths, A., Milne, R. and Cherryman, J. (2011) 'A question of control? The formulation of suspect and witness question strategies by advanced interviewers', *International Journal of Police Science and Management*, 13: 1–13.

Griffiths, A., Milne, R., Dando, C and Cherryman, J. (forthcoming). 'Is omni-competence possible? A comparison of advanced witness and suspect interviews carried out by the same interviewers', *Journal of Investigative Psychology and Offender Profiling*.

Groombridge, N. (2016) 'Making a murderer', *Criminology in Public*. Available at: http://criminologyinpublic.blogspot.co.uk/ (accessed 4 February 2017).

Grounds, A. (2004) 'Psychological consequences of wrongful conviction and imprisonment', *Canadian Journal of Criminology and Criminal Justice*, 46(2): 165–82.

Grounds, A. (2005) 'Understanding the effects of wrongful imprisonment', *Crime and Justice*, 32: 1–58.

Gudjonsson, G. (1993) 'Confession evidence, psychological vulnerabilities and expert testimony', *Journal of Community and Applied Social Psychology*, 3(2): 117–29.

Gudjonsson, G. (2003) *The psychology of interrogations and confessions: A handbook*, Chichester: Wiley.

Gudjonsson, G.H., Clare, I.C.H., Rutter, S. and Pearse, J. (1993) *Persons at risk during interviews in police custody: The identification of vulnerabilities*, Royal Commission on Criminal Justice, Research Study No. 12, London: HMSO.

Gudjonsson, G.H., Sigurdsson, J.F. and Sigfusdottir, I.D. (2009) 'Interrogations and false confessions among adolescents in seven countries in Europe: what background and psychological factors best discriminate between false confessors and non-false confessors?', *Psychology, Crime and Law*, 15: 711–28.

Hacking, I. (1995) *Rewriting the soul: Multiple personality and the sciences of memory*, Princeton, NJ: Princeton University Press.

Hall, A. (1994) 'It couldn't happen today?', in M. McConville and L. Bridges (eds) *Criminal justice in crisis*, Aldershot: Edward Elgar, pp 313–21.

Hall, C., Speechley, N. and Burnett, R. (2016) *The impact of being wrongly accused of abuse in occupations of trust: Victims' voices*, Oxford: University of Oxford.

Hancock, R. (1963) *Ruth Ellis: The last woman to be hanged*, London: Weidenfeld and Nicholson.

Hanson, C. (2011) 'The case of Eddie Gilfoyle and free speech'. Available at: http://www.insidetime.org/articleview.asp?a=889&c=the_case_of_eddie_gilfoyle_and_free_speech (accessed 1 December 2011).

Head, M. and Mann, S. (2009) *Law in perspective: Ethics, society and critical thinking*, Sydney: UNSW Press.

Helpmeinvestigate (no date) 'Home page'. Available at: http://helpmeinvestigate.com/tag/citizen-journalism/ (accessed 11 September 2011).

Hewson, B. (2014) 'Operation Yewtree: defaming the dead?', *Spiked*, 8 May. Available at: http://www.spiked-online.com/newsite/article/operation-yewtree-defaming-the-dead/14994#.V8WQNjWgEnM (accessed 25 August 2016).

Hill, P. (1996) *Forever lost: Forever gone*, London: Bloomsbury.

Hill, P. (2010) 'Paddy Hill was in trauma counselling for Birmingham Six ordeal', *The Guardian*, 19 October. Available at: https://www.theguardian.com/uk/2010/oct/19/paddy-hill-birmingham-six-counselling (accessed 23 June 2016).

Hill, P., Young, M. and Sargant, T. (1985) *More rough justice*, Middlesex: Penguin.

HMCPSI (Her Majesty's Crown Prosecution Service Inspectorate) and HMIC (Her Majesty's Inspectorate of Constabulary) (2015) 'Achieving best evidence in child sexual abuse cases'. Available at: https://www.justiceinspectorates.gov.uk/cjji/wp-content/uploads/sites/2/2014/12/CJJI_ABE_Dec14_rpt.pdf (accessed 28 August 2016).

Hobbs, D. (1997) 'Obituary: Iris Bentley', *The Independent*, 28 January. Available at: http://www.independent.co.uk/news/people/obituary-iris-bentley-1285561.html (accessed 12 June 2016).

Holmes, W. (2002) 'Who are the wrongly convicted on Death Row?', in S.D. Westervelt and J.A. Humphrey (eds) *Wrongly convicted: Perspectives on failed justice*, New Brunswick, NJ: Rutgers University Press, pp 99–113.

Home Affairs Select Committee (2002) *The conduct of investigations into past cases of abuse in children's homes*, HC 836-1, London: House of Commons.

Home Office (1985a) *Police and Criminal Evidence Act 1984*, London: HMSO.

Home Office (1985b) *Police and Criminal Evidence Act 1984 (s. 66), codes of practice*, London: HMSO.

Hopkins, S. (2016) 'Dozens of murderers launch appeals after Supreme Court decision on joint enterprise laws', *Huffington Post*, 21 June. Available at: http://www.huffingtonpost.co.uk/entry/joint-enterprise-supreme-court-decision-leads-to-dozens-of-appeals-being-launched_uk_576416c7e4b01fb658639478 (accessed 3 December 2016).

Hostettler, J. (1992) *The politics of criminal law: Reform in the nineteenth century*, London: Barry Rose Law Publishers.

Hostettler, J. (2009) *A history of criminal justice*, London: Waterside Press.

House of Commons Justice Committee (2015) *Criminal Cases Review Commission: Twelfth report of session 2014–15*, London: The Stationery Office.

Hucklesby, A. (2009) 'The prosecution process', in A. Hucklesby and A. Wahidin (eds) *Criminal justice*, Oxford: OUP, pp 61–82.

Huff, C.R. and Killias, M. (eds) (2013) *Wrongful convictions and miscarriages of justice: Causes and remedies in North American and European criminal justice systems*, New York, NY: Routledge.

Huff, C.R., Rattner, A. and Sagarin, E. (1986) 'Guilty until proven innocent: wrongful conviction and public policy', *Crime and Delinquency*, 32: 518–44.

Innocencenetwork (no date) 'Home page'. Available at: http:// innocencenetwork.org/ (accessed 24 July 2016).

Innocence Project (no date). Available at: http://www.innocenceproject. org/dna-exonerations-in-the-united-states/ (accessed 27 December 2016).

Innocent (no date) 'Home page'. Accessed 12 February 2009 (but no longer available) at: http://www.innocent.org.uk/

Insidejustice (no date) 'Home page'. Available at: http://www. insidejusticeuk.com/ (accessed 12 July 2016).

IPCC (Independent Police Complaints Commission) (2013) *Lynette White – IPCC Commissioner Overview*. Available at: www.ipcc.gov. uk/sites/default/files/Documents/guidelines_reports/L_White_ Foreword.PDF [note that the IPCC has now become the Independent Office for Police Conduct and some documents have disappeared from its websites. See broken links at: https://www.wired-gov.net/ wg/wg-news-1.nsf/0/7C60EDC9307D746B80257BF600494949? OpenDocument].

Irving, B. (1980) *Police interrogation. A case study of current practice*, Research Studies No. 2, London: HMSO.

Irving, B. and Dunninghan, C. (1993) *Human factors in the quality control of CID investigations*, Royal Commission on Criminal Justice, Research Study No. 21, London: HMSO.

Irving, B. and Hilgendorf, L. (1980) *Police interrogation: The psychological approach*, Research Studies No. 1, London: HMSO.

Irving, B. and McKenzie, I. (1989) *Police interrogation: The effects of the Police and Criminal Evidence Act 1984*, London: Police Foundation.

Jamieson, R. and Grounds, A. (2005) 'No sense of an ending? Researching the experience of imprisonment and release among Republican ex-prisoners', *Theoretical Criminology*, 7: 347–62.

Jenkins, S. (2013a) 'Secondary victims and the trauma of wrongful conviction: families' and children's perspectives on imprisonment, release and adjustment', *Australian and New Zealand Journal of Criminology*, 46(1): 119–37.

Jenkins, S. (2013b) 'Miscarriages of justice and the discourse of innocence: perspectives from appellants, campaigners, journalists and legal practitioners', *Journal of Law and Society*, 40(3): 329–55.

Jenkins, S. (2014) 'Families at war? Relationships between survivors of wrongful conviction and survivors of serious crime', *International Review of Victimology*, 20(2): 243–61.

Jenkins, S. (2015) 'How easy it is to convict the dead and defenceless', *The Guardian*, 5 August. Available at: http://www.theguardian.com/commentisfree/2015/aug/05/convict-dead-defenceless-case-edward-heath (accessed 22 July 2016).

Jessel, D. (2009) 'Innocence or safety: why the wrongly convicted are better served by safety', *The Guardian*, 15 December. Available at: https://www.theguardian.com/uk/2009/dec/15/prisons-and-probation (accessed 20 December 2016).

Jessell, D. (1994) *Trial and error*, London: Headline Book Publishing.

Johnston, E. (2015) 'The innocent cannot afford to plead not guilty', *Criminal Law and Justice Weekly*, 11 September. Available at: http://www.criminallawandjustice.co.uk/features/Innocent-Cannot-Afford-Plead-Not-Guilty (accessed 26 October 2016).

Joughin, L. and Morgan, E.M. (1948) *The legacy of Sacco and Vanzetti*, New Jersey, NJ: Princeton University Press.

Justice (no date) '*Nunn v Chief Constable of Suffolk Constabulary* [2014] UKSC 37'. Available at: https://justice.org.uk/nunn/ (accessed 13 June 2017).

Justice4kevinnunn.org.uk (no date) 'Home page'. Accessed 28 June 2016 (but no longer available) at: http://justice4kevinnunn.wronglyaccusedperson.org.uk/.

Kauzlarich, D., Matthews, R. and Miller, W. (2001) 'Towards a victimology of state crime', *Critical Criminology*, 10(3): 173–94.

Keane, A. (2006) *The modern law of evidence*, Oxford: Oxford University Press.

Kee, R. (1989) *Trial and error: The Maguires, the Guildford Four bombings and British justice*, London: Penguin.

Kennedy, H. (2004) *Just law: The changing face of justice and why it matters to us all*, London: Vintage Holmes.

Kennedy, L. (1961) *Ten Rillington Place*, London: Penguin.

Kerr, Lord (2013) 'Miscarriage of justice – when should an appellate court quash conviction?', JUSTICE Scotland International Human Rights Day Lecture. Available at: https://www.crimeline.info/news/miscarriage-of-justicewhen-should-an-appellate-court-quash-conviction (accessed 10 December 2016).

Klockars, C.B. (1980) 'The Dirty Harry problem', *Annals of the American Academy of Political and Social Science*, 452: 33–47.

Knoops, G. (2013) *Redressing miscarriages of justice: Practice and procedure in (international) criminal cases*, Leiden: Brill.

Koestler, A. (1956) *Reflections on hanging*, London: Victor Gollancz.

Lahiri, S. (1998) 'Uncovering Britain's South Asian past: the case of George Edalji', *Violence and abuse*, 6(1), 22–33.

Laming, H. (2003) *The Victoria Climbie inquiry*, London: Stationery Office.

Laville, S. (2011) 'What price? 14 years in jail for a murder conviction that was overturned', *The Guardian*, 8 May. Available at: https://www. theguardian.com/law/2011/may/08/14-years-murder-conviction-overturned (accessed 19 May 2015).

Laville, S. (2012) 'Criminal Cases Review Commission must be reformed, say campaigners', *The Guardian*, 27 March. Available at: http://www.guardian.co.uk/law/2012/mar/27/criminal-cases-review-commission-reform-campaign (accessed 12 April 2012).

Law Commission (1995) *Criminal law evidence in criminal proceedings: Hearsay and related topics – a consultation paper*, London: Law Commission.

Lean, S. (2007) *No smoke: The shocking truth about British justice*, Newcastle-Upon-Tyne: Exposure Publishing.

Leeney, D.G. and Muller-Johnson, K. (2011) 'Examining the forensic quality of police call centre interviews', *Psychology, Crime and Law*, 18: 669–88.

Leng, R. (1993) *The right to silence in police interrogation: A study of some of the issues underlying the debate research*, Royal Commission on Criminal Justice, Research Study No. 10, London: HMSO.

Leo, R. (2010) 'From false confession to wrongful conviction: seven psychological processes', *Journal of Psychiatry and the Law*, 38: 9–56.

Leo, R. and Drizin, S. (2010) 'The three errors: pathways to false confessions and wrongful conviction', in G. Lassiter and C. Meissner (eds) *Police interrogations and false confessions: Current research, practice and policy recommendations*, Washington, DC: American Psychological Association, pp 9–30.

Leo, R. and Ofshe, R. (1998) 'Consequences of false confessions: deprivations of liberty and miscarriages of justice in the age of psychological interrogation', *Journal of Criminal Law and Criminology*, 88(2): 429–96.

Leo, R. and Ofshe, R. (2001) 'The truth about false confessions and advocacy scholarship', *The Criminal Law Bulletin*, 37: 293–370.

Lester, A. (2016) 'Human rights must be protected against abuse of power', *The Guardian*, 16 May. Available at: https://www.theguardian. com/commentisfree/2016/may/16/human-rights-abuse-of-power-conservatives-bill-of-rights (accessed 6 February 2017).

Leverick, F. and Chalmers, J. (2014) 'Causes of wrongful conviction', in J. Chalmers, F. Leverick and A. Shaw (eds) *Post-corroboration safeguards review report of the academic expert group*, Edinburgh: The Scottish Government, pp 30–43.

Liberty (2006) *Quashing convictions*, London: Liberty.

Linehan, H. (2016) '"Serial" underlines public's fascination with murder', *The Irish Times*, 6 February. Available at: http://www.irishtimes.com/news/world/us/serial-underlines-public-s-fascination-with-murder-1.2524350 (accessed 12 February 2017).

Lipscombe, S. and Beard, J. (2015) *Miscarriages of justice: Compensation schemes (House of Commons Briefing Note SN/HA/2131)*, London: House of Commons Library.

Locker, M. (2016) 'Serial season two: why did the "must-listen show" suffer a sophomore slump?', *The Guardian*, 5 April. Available at: http://www.theguardian.com/tv-and-radio/2016/apr/05/serial-season-two-bowe-bergdahl-podcast (accessed 12 August 2016).

Lockley, M. (2014) 'Birmingham pub bombings survivor: "We will never get justice"', *Birmingham Mail*, 2 November. Available at: http://www.birminghammail.co.uk/news/midlands-news/birmingham-pub-bombings-survivor-we-8033435 (accessed 20 January 2015).

Loftus, E.G. (1979) *Eyewitness testimony*, Cambridge: Harvard University Press.

Loftus, E.G. (2013) 'The fiction of memory', *TED Talk*, June. Available at: http://www.ted.com/talks/elizabeth_loftus_the_fiction_of_memory?language=en-t-349000 (accessed 12 August 2016).

Lomax, S. (2011) 'The role of the Internet in fighting a miscarriage of justice', *Inside Justice*. Available at: http://www.insidejusticeuk.com/articles/the-role-of-the-internet-in-fighting-a-miscarriage-of-justice/14 (accessed 10 May 2016).

MacDonald, S., Snook, B. and Milne, R. (2016) 'Witness interview training: a field evaluation', *Journal of Police and Criminological Psychology* 32(1), 77–84.

Macpherson of Cluny, W., Sir (1999) *The Stephen Lawrence inquiry*, Cm 4262-1, London: HMSO.

Maguire, M. (2003) 'Criminal investigation and crime control', in T. Newburn (ed) *Handbook of policing*, Cullompton: Willan, pp 363–93.

Maguire, M. and Norris, C. (1993) *The conduct and supervision of criminal investigations*, Royal Commission on Criminal Justice, Research Study No. 5, London: HMSO.

Maguire, P. (2008) *My father's watch: The story of a child prisoner in 70s Britain*, London: Fourth Estate.

Mail Online (2005) 'Neighbour: "I tried to help battered Billie-Jo"'. Available at: www.dailymail.co.uk/news/article-346643/Neighbour-I-tried-help-battered-Billie-Jo.html (accessed 1 February 2018).

Malone, C. (2012) 'Shaken baby syndrome and the fight for justice', *The Justice Gap*, 1 August. Available at: http://thejusticegap.com/2012/08/shaken-baby-syndrome-and-the-fight-for-justice/ (accessed 23 May 2016).

Mansfield, M. (1993) *Presumed guilty: The British legal system exposed*, London: William Heinemann.

Martin, L. (2006) 'Satanic abuse: key witness says I lied', *The Observer*, 24 September. Available at: https://www.theguardian.com/uk/2006/sep/24/scotland (accessed 27 December 2015).

Matthews, R.A. (2004) 'Inference with legal evidence: common sense is necessary, but not sufficient', *Medicine, Science and the Law*, 44: 189–92.

May, J. (1994) *Report of the inquiry into the circumstances surrounding the convictions arising out of the bomb attacks in Guildford and Woolwich in 1974*, London: HMSO.

McBarnet, D. (1978) 'The Fisher Report on the Confait case: four issues', *Modern Law Review*, 41(4): 455–63.

McBarnet, D. (1981) *Conviction: The law, the state and the construction of justice*, London: Macmillan.

McCarthy, N. (2016) 'New Year shootings killers may win appeals after shock Supreme Court ruling on "joint enterprise" cases', *Birmingham Mail*, 18 February. Available at: http://www.birminghammail.co.uk/news/midlands-news/new-year-shootings-killers-win-10909948 (accessed 3 December 2016).

McCartney, C. and Roberts, S. (2012) 'Building institutions to address miscarriages of justice in England and Wales: mission accomplished?', *University of Cincinnatti Law Review*, 80(4): 1333–61.

McClenaghan, M. (2014) 'Joint enterprise: caught in the drift-net', *The Justice Gap*, 1 April. Available at: http://thejusticegap.com/2014/04/joint-enterprise-caught-drift-net/ (accessed 12 June 2016).

McConville, M. and Bridges, L. (1994) *Criminal justice in crisis*, Aldershot: Edward Elgar.

McConville, M. and Hodgson, J. (1993) *Custodial legal advice and the right to silence*, Royal Commission on Criminal Justice, Research Study No. 16, London: HMSO.

McConville, M. and Marsh, L. (2014) *Criminal judges: Legitimacy, courts and state-induced guilty pleas in Britain*, Cheltenham: Edward Elgar Publishing Ltd.

McConville, M., Sanders, A. and Leng, R. (1991) *The case for the prosecution: Police suspects and the construction of criminality*, London: Routledge.

McConville, M., Hodgson, J., Bridges, L. and Pavlovic, A. (1994) *Standing accused: The organisation and practices of criminal defence lawyers in Britain*, Oxford: Clarendon Press.

McKee, G. and Franey, R. (1988) *Timebomb: Irish bombers, English justice and the Guildford Four*, London: Bloomsbury.

McNair, B. (1998) *The sociology of journalism*, London: Edward Arnold.

McSmith, A. (2007) 'Miscarriage of justice corrected as jury finds man guilty of murder', *The Independent*, 13 November. Available at: http://www.independent.co.uk/news/uk/crime/miscarriage-of-justice-corrected-as-jury-finds-man-guilty-of-murder-400089.html (accessed 15 June 2016).

McVeigh, K. (2015) 'Three quarters of police forces letting down vulnerable victims watchdog', *The Guardian*, 14 December. Available at: https://www.theguardian.com/uk-news/2015/dec/14/two-thirds-of-police-forces-letting-down-vulnerable-victims-watchdog (accessed 22 August 2016).

Merchant, M. (2011) 'A poor defence', *The Justice Gap*. Available at: http://thejusticegap.com/2011/11/poor-defence/ (accessed 20 December 2016).

Miller, S. (2005) *Victims as offenders: The paradox of women's' violence in relationships*, New Brunswick, NJ: Rutgers University Press.

Mills, H. (1992) 'Hanged man's sister sees hopes shattered', *The Independent*, 1 October. Available at: http://www.independent.co.uk/news/uk/hanged-mans-sister-sees-hopes-shattered-iris-bentleys-brother-derek-who-was-executed-almost-40-years-1554859.html (accessed 16 May 2016).

Milne, R. (2016) 'Let them be heard: enabling communication and recall of forensic interviewees', inaugural lecture, 22 June, University of Portsmouth, UK.

Milne, R. and Bull, R. (1999) *Investigative interviewing: Psychology and practice*, Chichester: Wiley.

Milne, R. and Bull, R. (2016) 'Witness interviews and crime investigation', in D. Groome and M. Eysenck (eds) *An introduction to applied cognitive psychology*, London: Psychology Press, pp 175–96.

Moffett, L. (2014) *Justice for victims before the International Criminal Court*, Oxon: Routledge.

MOJUK (Miscarriage of Justice UK) (no date) 'Start campaigning booklet'. Available at: http://www.mojuk.org.uk/justice/Campaign%20leaflett.pdf (accessed 20 June 2012).

Mole, C. (2012) 'Free to go? Surviving a wrongful conviction', *The Justice Gap*, 18 April. Available at: http://thejusticegap.com/2012/04/free-to-go-life-on-the-outside-for-the-wrongly-accused/ (accessed 20 July 2015).

Moody, O. (2012) 'Police got boy suspect drunk on cider', *The Times*, 17 January. Available at: http://www.thetimes.co.uk/tto/news/uk/crime/article3288748.ece (accessed 24 February 2014).

Moore, C. (2013) 'Treating every allegation against Jimmy Savile as a "fact" undermines justice', *The Telegraph*, 11 January. Available at: http://www.telegraph.co.uk/news/uknews/crime/jimmy-savile/9795920/Treating-every-allegation-against-Jimmy-Savile-as-a-fact-undermines-justice.html (accessed 12 August 2016).

Morrell, J. (1999) *No smoke without fire: A guide for victims of miscarriages of justice*, London: United Against Injustice.

Morris, N. (2015) 'Miscarriages of justice will result from fresh cuts to legal aid budget, say solicitors', *The Independent*, 10 June. Available at: http://www.independent.co.uk/news/uk/politics/miscarriages-of-justice-will-result-from-fresh-cuts-to-legal-aid-budget-say-solicitors-10311240.html (accessed 20 November 2015).

Morrison, S. (2013) 'Second ordeal for Sam months after jail release', *The Independent*, 25 June. Available at: http://www.independent.co.uk/news/uk/crime/second-ordeal-for-sam-hallam-months-after-jail-release-8673738.html (accessed 1 March 2015).

Morton, J. (2015) *Justice denied: Extraordinary miscarriages of justice*, London: Robinson.

Moston, S. and Engelberg, T. (1993) 'Police questioning techniques in tape recorded interviews with criminal suspects', *Policing and Society*, 3(3): 223–37.

Moston, S. and Stephenson, G.M. (1993) *The questioning and interviewing of suspects outside the police station*, Royal Commission on Criminal Justice, Research Study No. 22, London: HMSO.

Mulhall, J. (2016) 'Irishman Victor Nealon who wrongfully served 17 years in British prison for rape denied compensation', *The Irish Post*, 12 April. Available at: http://irishpost.co.uk/irishman-victor-nealon-wrongfully-served-17-years-british-prison-rape-denied-compensation/ (accessed 24 June 2016).

Mullin, C. (1990) *Error of judgement: The truth about the Birmingham bombings*, Dublin: Poolbeg.

Mumford, G. (2016) 'Making a murderer: the Netflix documentary beating TV drama at its own game', *The Guardian*, 7 January. Available at: https://www.theguardian.com/tv-and-radio/tvandradioblog/2016/jan/07/making-a-murderer-the-netflix-documentary-beating-tv-drama-at-its-own-game (accessed 29 August 2016).

Naughton, M. (2001) 'Wrongful convictions: towards a zemiological analysis of the tradition of criminal justice system reform', *Radical Statistics*, 76: 50–65.

Naughton, M. (2003) 'How big is the iceberg? A zemiological approach to quantifying miscarriages of justice', *Radical Statistics*, 81(5): 5–17.

Naughton, M. (2005) 'Redefining miscarriages of justice: a revived human-rights approach to unearth subjugated discourses of wrongful criminal conviction', *British Journal of Criminology*, 45(2): 165–82.

Naughton, M. (2006) 'Wrongful convictions and innocence projects in the UK: help, hope, and education', *Web Journal of Current Legal Issues*, 3. Available at: http://webjcli.ncl.ac.uk/2006/issue3/naughton3.html (accessed 2 May 2007).

Naughton, M. (2007) *Rethinking miscarriages of justice: Beyond the tip of the iceberg*, Basingstoke: Palgrave Macmillan.

Naughton, M. (2011) 'How the presumption of innocence renders the innocent vulnerable to wrongful convictions', *Irish Journal of Legal Studies*, 2(1): 40–54.

Naughton, M. (2012) *The Criminal Cases Review Commission: Hope for the innocent?*, Basingstoke: Palgrave Macmillan.

Naughton, M. (2013) *The innocent and the criminal justice system: A sociological analysis*, Basingstoke: Palgrave Macmillan.

Naughton, M. and Tan, G. (2010) *Claims of innocence: An introduction to wrongful convictions and how they might be challenged*, Bristol: University of Bristol.

Newby, M. (2012) 'Savile, Bryn Estyn and the danger of modern witch-hunts', *The Justice Gap*, 8 November. Available at: http://thejusticegap.com/2012/11/savile-bryn-estyn-and-the-danger-of-modern-witch-hunts/ (accessed 25 August 2016).

Newby, M. (2015) 'Challenging miscarriages of justice', *BFMS*. Available at: http://bfms.org.uk/challenging-miscarriages-of-justice/ (accessed 14 October 2015).

Newby, M. (2016) 'It's not for the police to decide a case, they are supposed to collect evidence', *The Justice Gap*, 15 February. Available at: http://thejusticegap.com/2016/02/12516/ (accessed 17 August 2016).

Neyroud, P. (2008) 'European Convention on Human Rights (ECHR)', in T. Newburn and P. Neyroud (eds) *Dictionary of policing*, Cullompton: Willan, pp 98–9.

Neyroud, P. and Beckley, A. (2001) *Policing, ethics and human rights*, Cullompton: Willan.

Nobles, R. and Schiff, D. (2000) *Understanding Miscarriages of Justice: Law, the Media, and the Inevitability of Crisis*, Oxford: Oxford University Press.

Nobles, R. and Schiff, D. (2009) 'Public confidence in criminal justice: the lessons from miscarriages of justice', *Howard Journal of Criminal Justice*, 48(5): 461–71.

Nurse, A. (2012) 'Evolution not revolution', in J. Robins (ed) *Wrongly accused: Who is responsible for investigating miscarriages of justice?*, London: Wilmington Press, pp 69–72.

Oates, J. (2013) *John Christie of Rillington Place: Biography of a serial killer*, London: Pen and Sword Books.

O'Brien, M. (2009) *The death of justice: Guilty until proven innocent*, Ceredigion: Y Lolfa.

Office of the High Commissioner for Human Rights (1990) 'Basic principles on the role of lawyers', adopted by the 8th United Nations Congress on the Prevention of Crime and the Treatment of Offenders, Havana, Cuba.

Oldfield, R. (2010) *Outrage: The Edalji Five and the shadow of Sherlock Holmes*, London: Vanguard Press.

O'Neil, E. (2011) 'Rebalancing the scales?', *Political Insight*, 2(2): 26–8.

Orfield, L.B. (1937) 'Criminal appeals: technicality and prejudicial error', *Journal of Criminal Law and Criminology*, 27(5): 668–95.

Oxford English Dictionary (no date) 'Victim'. Available at: http://www.oxforddictionaries.com/definition/english/victim (accessed 24 June 2016).

Packer, H. (1968) *The limits of criminal sanctions*, Stanford, CA: Stanford University Press.

PAFAA (People Against False Accusations of Abuse) (no date) 'Falsely accused of sexual abuse?'. Available at: http://www.pafaa.org.uk/wordpress/ (accessed 12 June 2016).

Paris, J. (1991) *Scapegoat! The inside story of the trial of Derek Bentley*, London: Duckworth.

Parliament (2014) 'Joint enterprise: follow-up – Justice Committee'. Available at: http://www.publications.parliament.uk/pa/cm201415/cmselect/cmjust/310/31006.htm (accessed 23 December 2016).

Patten, C. (1999) *A new beginning: Policing in Northern Ireland: The report of the Independent Commission on Policing for Northern Ireland*, London: HMSO.

Pattenden, R. (1996) *English criminal appeals 1844–1994*, Oxford: Clarendon.

Peachey, P. (2013) 'Collapse of Britain's biggest police corruption trial: "No misconduct involved" in Cardiff Three fit-up case', *The Independent*, 16 July. Available at: http://www.independent.co.uk/news/uk/crime/collapse-of-britain-s-biggest-police-corruption-trial-no-misconduct-involved-in-cardiff-three-fit-up-8711679.html (accessed 28 July 2017).

Peachey, P. (2015) 'Privatisation of forensic services "threat to justice" and putting the work in police hands would be "disastrous," warn experts', *The Independent*, 21 January. Available at: http://www.independent.co.uk/news/uk/crime/privatisation-of-forensic-services-a-threat-to-justice-and-putting-the-work-in-police-hands-would-be-9991356.html (accessed 25 October 2016).

Pescod, L., Wilcock, R. and Milne, R. (2013) 'Improving eyewitness memory in police call centre interviews', *Policing: A Journal of Policy and Practice*, 7: 299–306.

Petrosian, D. (2014) 'A study of citizen journalism: challenging the official truth?', unpublished BA Criminal Justice thesis, University of Kent, UK.

Picinali, F. (2015) 'The threshold lies in the method: instructing jurors about reasoning beyond reasonable doubt', *International Journal of Evidence and Proof*, 19(3): 139–53.

Poyser, S. (2012) 'Watchdogs of the wrongly convicted: the role of the media in revealing miscarriages of justice', unpublished PhD thesis, University of Portsmouth, UK.

Poyser, S. (2016) 'Ruined lives: identifying and responding to the harms of wrongful conviction', paper presented at the British Society of Criminology Conference, Nottingham, 6–8 July.

Poyser, S. (forthcoming) 'Unofficial responses to miscarriages of justice: the role of the media', in S. Poyser, A. Nurse and R. Milne (eds) *Miscarriages of justice: Contemporary perspectives*, Surrey: Ashgate.

Poyser, S. and Grieve, J. (forthcoming) 'Miscarriages of justice: what can we learn?', in Milne, R. and Griffiths, A. (eds) *Investigation: Psychology into practice*, London: Routledge.

Poyser, S. and Milne, R. (2011) 'Miscarriages of justice: a call for continued research focussing on reforming the investigative process', *British Journal of Forensic Practice*, 13(2): 61–71.

Poyser, S. and Milne, R. (2015) 'No grounds for complacency and plenty for continued vigilance: miscarriages of justice as drivers for research on reforming the investigative process', *Policing: Journal of Policy, Practice and Principles*, 88(3): 1–16.

Price, C. and Caplan, J. (1977) *The Confait confessions*, London: Marion Boyars.

Price, J. (2016) 'Dear Michael Gove, now you have some time on your hands …', *The Justice Gap*, 8 July. Available at: http://thejusticegap. com/2016/07/dear-michael-gove-now-time-hands/ (accessed 22 August 2016).

Quinney, R. (1972) 'Who is the victim?', *Criminology*, 10(3): 323–41.

Quirk, H. (2007) 'Identifying miscarriages of justice: why Innocence in the UK is not the answer', *Modern Law Review*, 70(5): 759–77.

Quirk, H. (2017) *The rise and fall of the right of silence*, Abingdon: Routledge.

Radin, E.D. (1964) *The innocents*, New York, NY: Morrow.

Radzinowicz, L. and Hood, R. (1986) *A history of English criminal law, volume 5: The emergence of penal policy*, London: Stevens & Son.

Rasch, W. (1981) 'The effects of indeterminate detention: a study of men sentenced to life imprisonment', *International Journal of Law and Psychology*, 4: 417–31.

RCCJ (Royal Commission on Criminal Justice) (1993) *Report (Cmnd 2263)*, London: HMSO.

RCCP (Royal Commission on Criminal Procedure) (1981) *Report (Cmnd 8092)*, London: HMSO.

Reiner, R. (2000) *The politics of the police*, Oxford: Oxford University Press.

Riccardelli, R., Bell, J. and Clow, K.A. (2012) 'Now I see it for what it really is: the impact of participation on an innocence project practicum on Criminology students', *Albany Law Review*, 75: 1439–66.

Richardson, J. (2016) *Criminal Law Week*, issue 7, 22 February.

Roberts, J. (2003) 'Too little too late: ineffective assistance of counsel, the duty to investigate, and pre-trial discovery in criminal cases', *Fordham Urban Law Journal*, 31(4): 1097–155.

Roberts, S. (2003) '"Unsafe" convictions: defining and compensating miscarriages of justice', *The Modern Law Review*, 66(3): 441–51.

Roberts, K. (2012) 'Police interviewing of criminal suspects', *Internet Journal of Criminology*, December. Available at: http://www. internetjournalofcriminology.com/roberts_police_interview_ criminal_suspects_ijc_dec_2012.pdf

Robins, J. (2011) 'Righting New Labour's wrong to victims of miscarriages of justice', *The Guardian*, 8 July. Available at: http://www.guardian.co.uk/law/2011/jul/08/campaign-for-victims-of-miscarriages-of-justice (accessed 10 July 2011).

Robins, J. (ed) (2012) *Wrongly accused: Who is responsible for investigating miscarriages of justice?*, London: The Justice Gap.

Robins, J. (2015a) 'Wrongly convicted men launch new case against the justice secretary', *The Independent*, 18 January. Available at: http://www.independent.co.uk/news/uk/home-news/wrongly-convicted-men-launch-new-case-against-the-justice-secretary-9985773.html (accessed 19 January 2015).

Robins, J. (2015b) 'Justice watchdog sued by wrongly convicted man who spent 17 years in prison for attempted rape', *The Independent*, 15 March. Available at: http://www.independent.co.uk/news/uk/home-news/justice-watchdog-sued-by-wrongly-convicted-man-who-spent-17-years-in-prison-for-attempted-rape-10108752.html (accessed 16 March 2015).

Robins, J. (2016a) 'Rough justice', *New Law Journal*, 2 June. Available at: http://www.newlawjournal.co.uk/nlj/content/rough-justice-0 (accessed 25 June 2016).

Robins, J. (2016b) 'Washing hands of justice?', *Criminal Law and Justice Weekly*, 180(16). Available at: https://www.criminallawandjustice.co.uk/comment/Washing-Hands-Justice (accessed 18 December 2016).

Robins, J. (2017) 'It is far too easy for innocent people to be falsely accused', *The Justice Gap*. Available at: http://thejusticegap.com/2017/03/far-easy-innocent-people-falsely-accused/ (accessed 10 April 2017).

Robins, R. (2014) *The first miscarriage of justice: The unreported and amazing case of Tony Stock*, Hampshire: Waterside Press.

Rock, F. (2001) 'The genesis of a witness statement', *Forensic Linguistics*, 8: 44–72.

Rose, D. (1996) *In the name of the law: The collapse of criminal justice*, London: Vintage.

Rozenberg, G. (1992) 'Miscarriages of justice', in E. Stockdale and S. Casale (eds) *Criminal justice under stress*, London: Blackstone, pp 23–35.

Rozenberg, G. (2016) 'Correcting the joint enterprise law won't lead to mass prison releases', *The Guardian*, 18 February. Available at: https://www.theguardian.com/commentisfree/2016/feb/18/joint-entreprise-law-corrected-prison-releases-uk-supreme-court (accessed 3 December 2016).

Ryan, B. (1977) *The poisoned life of Mrs Maybrick*, London: Penguin.

Salman, S. (2013) 'Legal aid cuts: "a return to widespread miscarriages of justice"', *The Guardian*, 2 July. Available at: http://www.theguardian.com/society/2013/jul/02/legal-aid-cuts-widespread-miscarriages-justice?commentpage=1 (accessed 15 June 2015).

Samhallam (no date) 'Home page'. Available at: http://www.samhallam.com/ (accessed 12 May 2016).

Sanders, A., Burton, M. and Young, R. (2010) *Criminal justice*, Oxford: OUP.

Sanders, G.S. (1986) 'The usefulness of eyewitness research from the perspective of police investigators', unpublished manuscript, State University of New York, USA.

Sapsford, R.J. (1978) 'Life sentence prisoners: psychological changes during sentence', *British Journal of Criminology*, 18: 128–45.

Savage, S. and Milne, R. (2007) 'Miscarriages of justice', in T. Newburn, T. Williamson and A. Wright (eds) *Handbook of criminal investigation*, Devon: Willan, pp 610–27.

Savage, S., Poyser, S. and Grieve, J. (2007) 'Putting wrongs to rights: campaigns against miscarriages of justice', *Criminology and Criminal Justice*, 7(1): 83–105.

Scheck, B., Neufeld, P. and Dwyer, J. (2000) *Actual innocence: Five days to execution and other dispatches from the wrongly convicted*, New York, NY: Doubleday.

Seabrook, V. (2016) 'Miscarriage of justice victim Sam Hallam takes compensation battle to Supreme Court', *Hackney Citizen*, 28 April. Available at: http://hackneycitizen.co.uk/2016/04/28/miscarriage-justice-victim-sam-hallam-compensation-supreme-court/ (accessed 24 August 2016).

Sedley, S. (2011) *Ashes and sparks: Essays on law and justice*, Cambridge: Cambridge University Press.

Sekar, S. (1998) *Fitted in: The Cardiff Three and the Lynette White inquiry*, London: The Fitted-In Project.

Sekar, S. (2013) *The Cardiff Five: Innocent beyond any doubt*, London: Waterside Press.

Sellin, T. and Wolfgang, M. (1964) *The measurement of delinquency*, New York, NY: Wiley.

Seneviratne, M. (2000) 'Ombudsman 2000', *Nottingham Law Journal*, 9(1): 13–24.

Shaikh, T. (2007) 'Sally Clark, mother wrongly convicted of killing her sons found dead at home', *The Guardian*, 17 March. Available at: http://www.theguardian.com/society/2007/mar/17/childrensservices.uknews (accessed 15 June 2016).

Shepherd, E. (1993) *Aspects of police interviewing: Issues in criminological and legal psychology*, Leicester: BPS.

Shepherd, E. and Griffiths, A. (2013) *Investigative interviewing: The conversation management approach*, Oxford: OUP.

Shepherd, E. and Milne, R. (1999) 'Full and faithful: ensuring quality practice and integrity of outcome in witness interviews', in A. Heaton-Armstrong, D. Wolchover and E. Shepherd (eds) *Analysing witness testimony*, London: Blackstone Press, pp 124–55.

Shepherd, E. and Milne, R. (2006) 'Have you told the management about this? Bringing witness interviewing into the 21st century', in A. Heaton-Armstrong, E, Shepherd, G. Gudjonsson, and D. Wolchover (eds) *Witness testimony: Psychological, investigative, and evidential perspectives*, Oxford: Oxford University Press, pp 131–52.

Shorter, L. (2013) 'Justice at last', *Inside Time*, 1 October. Available at: http://www.insidejusticeuk.com/articles/justice-at-last/31 (accessed 22 August 2016).

Simon, R.J. and Blaskovich, D.A. (2007) *A comparative analysis of capital punishment: Statutes, policies, frequencies and public attitudes the world over*, New York, NY: Lexington.

Sims, G.R. (2012) *Two kings' pardons: The martyrdom of Adolf Beck*, London: Gale.

Slapper, G. and Kelly, D. (2012) *The English legal system*, London: Routledge.

Smith, C. (2016) 'Miscarriage compensation fight goes to Supreme Court', *Law Society Gazette*. Accessed 20 December 2016 (but no longer available) at: https://www.lawgazette.co.uk/law/miscarriage-compensation-fight-goes-to-supreme-court/5054721

Smith, D.J. (1983) *Police and people in London: A survey of Londoners*, London: Policy Studies Institute.

Smith, N.M. (2016) 'Making a murderer directors defend series: "Of course we left out evidence"', *The Guardian*, 18 January. Available at: https://www.theguardian.com/culture/2016/jan/17/making-a-murderer-netflix-steven-avery (accessed 18 August 2016).

Softley, P. (1981) *Police interrogation: An observational study in four police stations*, Royal Commission on Criminal Procedure, Research Study No 4, Cmnd 8092, London: HMSO.

Soukara, S., Bull, R., Virj, A., Turner, M. and Cherryman, J. (2009) 'What really happens in police interviews of suspects? Tactics and confessions', *Psychology, Crime and Law*, 15: 493–506.

Starmer, K. (2016) 'Victims of crimes are ill-served by the justice system: this Bill will change that', *The Guardian*, 25 January. Available at: http://www.theguardian.com/commentisfree/2016/jan/25/crime-victims-bill-poppi-worthington-police-prosecutors (accessed 24 August 2016).

Steer, D. (1981) *Uncovering crime: The police role*, Royal Commission on Criminal Procedure, Research Study No. 7, Cmnd 8092, London: HMSO.

Stelfox, P. (2007) 'Professionalising criminal investigation', in T. Newburn, T. Williamson and A. Wright (eds) *Handbook of criminal investigation*, Cullompton: Willan, pp 628–51.

Stelfox, P. (2011) 'Criminal investigation: filling the skills gap in leadership, management, and supervision', *Policing*, 5(1): 15–22.

Stephens, M. and Hill, P. (1999) 'The role and impact of the media', in C. Walker and K. Starmer (eds) *Miscarriages of justice: A review of justice in error*, Oxford: OUP, pp 236–88.

Stevens, D.J. (2010) *Introduction to American policing*, Sudbury, MA: Jones and Bartlett.

Stone, R. (2010) *Textbook on civil liberties and human rights*, Oxford: Oxford University Press

Stratton, G. (2014) 'Wrongfully convicting the innocent: a state crime?', *Critical Criminology*, 23: 21–37.

Syal, R. (2016) 'Justice system is failing witnesses and victims of crime say MPs', *The Guardian*, 27 May. Available at: https://www.theguardian.com/uk-news/2016/may/27/justice-system-failing-witnesses-victims-crime (accessed 22 August 2016).

Sykes, G.M. (1958) *The society of captives: A study of maximum security prison*, Princeton, NJ: Princeton University Press.

Tan, G. (2010) 'Structuration theory and wrongful imprisonment: from "victimhood" to "survivorship"?', *Critical Criminology*, 19(3): 175–96.

Taylor, N. and Wood, J. (1999) 'Victims of miscarriages of justice', in C. Walker and K. Starmer (eds) *Miscarriages of justice: A review of justice in error*, Oxford: OUP, pp 247–62.

The Guardian (2016) 'Making a murderer subject's half-brother releases rap track: they didn't do it', 13 January. Available at: https://www.theguardian.com/music/2016/jan/13/making-a-murderer-netflix-half-brother-brad-dassey-rap-track-they-didnt-do-it (accessed 12 August 2016).

Thompson, W. and Shumann, E.L. (1987) 'Interpretation of statistical evidence in criminal trials: the prosecutor's fallacy and the defense attorney's fallacy', *Law and Human Behavior*, 2(3): 167.

Tibbetts, G. (2008) 'Babysitter wins appeal over toddler murder conviction', *The Telegraph*, 1 May. Available at: http://www.telegraph.co.uk/news/1917082/Babysitter-wins-appeal-over-toddler-murder-conviction.html (accessed 17 June 2016).

Timm, T. (2016) 'Making a murderer depicts miscarriages of justice that are not at all rare', *The Guardian*, 6 January. Available at: https://www.theguardian.com/commentisfree/2016/jan/06/making-a-murder-netflix-series-miscarriages-of-justice-are-not-at-all-rare (accessed 24 August 2016).

Townsend, M. (2011) 'Police warned about rising risk of false confessions', *The Guardian*, 9 October. Available at: https://www.theguardian.com/uk/2011/oct/09/false-confessions-sean-hodgson-courts (accessed 9 October 2011).

Townsend, M. and Asthana, A. (2009) 'Sara Payne calls for major overhaul of the criminal justice system', *The Observer*, 1 November. Available at: http://www.theguardian.com/politics/2009/nov/01/sara-payne-overhaul-justice-system (accessed 12 May 2016).

Turnbull, G. (2011) *Trauma*, London: Bantam Press.

Turner, B. and Rennell, T. (1995) *When daddy came home: How family life changed forever in 1945*, London: Hutchinson.

Vollertson, N. (2012) 'Wrongful conviction: how a family survives', *Albany Law Review*, 75(3): 1509–28.

Wadham, J. and Mountfield, H. (1999) *Blackstone's guide to the Human Rights Act 1998*, London: Blackstone Press Ltd.

Walker, C. (1999) 'Miscarriages of justice in principle and practice', in C. Walker and K. Starmer (eds) *Miscarriages of justice: A review of justice in error*, London: Blackstone, pp 31–62.

Walker, C. and McCartney, C. (2008) 'Criminal justice and miscarriages of justice in England and Wales', in C. Huff and M. Killias (eds) *Wrongful convictions: International perspectives*, Philadelphia, PA: Temple University Press, pp 183–212.

Walker, C. and Starmer, K. (eds) (1999) *Miscarriages of justice: A review of justice in error*, London: Blackstone.

Walsh, D. and Bull, R. (2010) 'What really is effective in interviews with suspects? A study comparing interviewing skills against interviewing outcomes', *Legal and Criminal Psychology*, 15: 305–21.

Walsh, D., O-Callaghan, S. and Milne, R. (2016) 'Questioning the interrogational practices of US law-enforcement officers', in A. Kapardis and D. Farrington (eds) *The psychology of crime, policing and courts*, London and New York, NY: Routledge, pp 119–35.

Weaver, G. (2006) *Conan Doyle and the parson's son: The case of George Edalji*, Cambridge: Vanguard Press.

Webster, R. (2009) *The secret of Bryn Estyn: The making of a modern witch-hunt*, Oxford: Orwell Press.

Westervelt, S.D. and Cook, S.J. (2010) 'Framing innocents: the wrongly convicted as victims of state harm', *Crime, Law, and Social Change*, 53: 259–75.

Westervelt, S.D. and Cook, S.J. (2012) 'Revealing the impact and aftermath of miscarriages of justice', *Albany Law Review*, 75(3): 1223–630.

Westervelt, S.D. and Cook, S.J. (2013) 'Life after exoneration: examining the aftermath of a wrongful capital conviction', in C.R. Huff and M. Killias (eds) *Wrongful convictions and miscarriages of justice: Causes and remedies in North American and European criminal justice systems*, New York, NY: Routledge, pp 261–82.

Weston, K. (2016) 'Dwaine George: How Cardiff Law School's Innocence Project discovered scientific evidence was of "no evidential significance"', *The Independent*, 3 February. Available at: http://www. independent.co.uk/student/news/dwaine-george-how-cardiff-law-school-s-innocence-project-discovered-scientific-evidence-was-of-no-a6850346.html (accessed 24 August 2016).

White, M. (2016) 'Child abuse claims: why due process and a fair hearing matter', *The Guardian*, 8 February. Available at: http://www. theguardian.com/society/blog/2016/feb/08/child-abuse-claims-why-due-process-and-a-fair-hearing-matter (accessed 22 August 2016).

Whittington-Egan, R. (2001) *The Oscar Slater murder story*, London: Neil Wilson Publishing.

Wilcock, R., Bull, R. and Milne, R. (2008) *Criminal identification by witnesses: Psychology and practice*, Oxford: Oxford University Press.

Williams, A. (2015) *Forensic criminology*, London: Routledge.

Williamson, T. (1994) 'Reflections on current police practice', in D. Morgan and G. Stephenson (eds) *Suspicion and silence: The rights of silence in criminal investigations*, London: Blackstone, pp 107–16.

Williamson, T., Milne, R. and Savage, S. (2013) *International developments in investigative interviewing*, London: Routledge.

Wiseman, E. (2016) 'The mother of all murder stories', *The Guardian*, 10 January. Available at: https://www.theguardian.com/lifeandstyle/2016/jan/10/why-making-a-murderer-is-compulsive-viewing (accessed 24 August 2016).

Witsjusticeproject.com (no date) 'WITs justice project: free the innocent'. Available at: http://www.witsjusticeproject.co.za/ (accessed 24 August 2016).

Woffinden, B. (1987) *Miscarriages of justice*, London: Hodder and Stoughton.

Woffinden, B. (2004) 'More cases in doubt as abuse verdict quashed', *The Guardian*, 6 February. Available at: https://www.theguardian.com/society/2004/feb/06/childrensservices.politics (accessed 24 August 2016).

Woffinden, B. (2010) 'The CCRC has failed', *The Guardian*, 30 November. Available at: http://www.guardian.co.uk/commentisfree/libertycentral/2010/nov/30/criminal-cases-review-commission-failed (accessed 30 November 2010).

Wright, R. and Powell, M.B. (2006) 'Investigative interviewers' perceptions of their difficulty in adhering to open-ended questions with child witnesses', *International Journal of Police Science & Management*, 8(4): 316–25.

Yant, M. (1991) *Presumed guilty: When innocent people are wrongly convicted*, London: Prometheus Books.

Young, M. (2015) *Opposable truths*, London: Matador.

Zander, M. (2013) 'Only the innocent need apply for compensation for a miscarriage of justice', *Criminal Law and Justice Weekly*, 177(2). Available at: https://www.criminallawandjustice.co.uk/features/Only-Innocent-Need-Apply-Compensation-Miscarriage-Justice (accessed 13 February 2018).

Zander, M. and Henderson, P. (1993) *The Crown Court study*, Royal Commission on Criminal Justice, Research Study No. 19, London: HMSO.

Zdenkowski, G. (1993) 'Remedies for miscarriage of justice: wrongful imprisonment', *Current Issues in Criminal Justice*, 5(1): 105–10.

Zellick, M. (2010) 'The causes of miscarriages of justice', *Medico-Legal Journal*, 78(1): 11–20.

List of court cases

Airey v Ireland [1979] Application No. 6289/73, [1979] ECHR 3, (1980) 2 EHRR 305.

Benham v UK [1996] 22 EHRR 293.

Chan Wing-Siu v The Queen [1985] 1 AC 168.

Goddi v Italy [1984] (Application No. 8966/80).

Granger v UK [1990] 12 EHRR 469.

Khan v the United Kingdom (Application No. 35394/97), ECHR 2000-V.

McInnes v Her Majesty's Advocate [2010] UKSC 7, 2010 SC (UKSC) 28.

Morris v the CCRC [2011] EHHC 117.

Mullen [2002] EWHC 230.

Nunn v Chief Constable of Suffolk Constabulary [2014] UKSC 37.

R (Adams) v Secretary of State [2009] EWHC 156 (Admin).

R (Adams) v Secretary of State for Justice [2011] UKSC 18.

R (Ebrahim) v Feltham Magistrates' Court; *Mouat v DPP* [2001] 2 Cr App R 23.

Re Fletcher's Application [1970] 2 All ER 527.

Regina v Powell and English [1999] 1 AC 1.

R (Hallam and Nealon) v Secretary of State for Justice [2016] EWCA Civ 355.

R (on the application of Nunn) (Appellant) v Chief Constable of Suffolk Constabulary and another (Respondents) [2014] UKSC 37.

R v Abadom [1983] 1 All ER 364.

R v Birmingham and Others [1992] Crim LR 117.

R v Clark (Sally) [1999] (unreported).

R v Davis, Rowe and Johnson [2001] 1 Cr App R 8.

R v Graham [1997] 1 Cr App R 302.

R v H and C [2004] 2 AC 134.

R v Jenkins (Sion David Charles) 98/4720/W3.

R v Jogee [2016] UKSC 8.

R v Silverlock [1894] 2 QB 766.

R v The CCRC, ex parte Pearson [1999] EWHC (Admin) 452 [2000].

Salduz v Turkey 36391/02 [2008] ECHR 1542.

Sofris v S [2004] Crim LR 846.

Index